L
Fred Le Savage
1020 East Ave.
Tomah, WI 54660

S0-BDG-067

Heroes are people who put themselves at risk for the benefit of others.

—OLIVER NORTH

ALSO BY OLIVER NORTH

Heroes Proved

American Heroes in Special Operations

American Heroes in the Fight Against Radical Islam

The Assassins

War Stories III

War Stories II

A Greater Freedom (editor)

War Stories

The Jericho Sanction

True Freedom

Mission Compromised

Under Fire

Real heroes don't wear spandex leotards and capes.

My heroes wear combat boots, flak jackets, and flight suits.

—OLIVER NORTH

OLIVER NORTH
WITH BOB HAMER

AMERICAN HEROES ON THE HOMEFRONT

The Hearts of Heroes

THRESHOLD EDITIONS
NEW YORK LONDON TORONTO SYDNEY NEW DELHI

Threshold Editions
A Division of Simon & Schuster, Inc.
1230 Avenue of the Americas
New York, NY 10020

First Threshold Editions hardcover edition November 2013

THRESHOLD EDITIONS and colophon are trademarks of Simon & Schuster, Inc.

For information about special discounts for bulk purchases,
please contact Simon & Schuster Special Sales at
1-866-506-1949 or business@simonandschuster.com.

The Simon & Schuster Speakers Bureau can bring authors to your live event.
For more information or to book an event, contact the Simon & Schuster Speakers
Bureau at 1-866-248-3049 or visit our website at www.simonspeakers.com.

Designed by Ruth Lee-Mui

Manufactured in the United States of America

1 3 5 7 9 10 8 6 4 2

Library of Congress Cataloging-in-Publication Data

North, Oliver.
American heroes on the homefront : the hearts of heroes /
Oliver North and Bob Hamer. — First Threshold Editions hardcover edition.
pages cm
1. Iraq War, 2003–2011—Veterans—United States—Biography.
2. Iraq War, 2003–2011—Veterans—United States—Pictorial works.
3. Afghan War, 2001—Veterans—United States—Biography.
4. Afghan War, 2001—Veterans—United States—Pictorial works.
5. Veterans—United States—Biography. 6. Veterans—United States—Pictorial works.
I. Hamer, Bob. II. Title.
DS79.766.A1N67 2013
956.7044'30922—dc23 2013019426

ISBN 978-1-4767-1432-5
ISBN 978-1-4767-1437-0 (ebook)

☆

For Betsy

My mate, my muse, my hero

Those who volunteer to serve in this long war

are the best and bravest of their generation.

—OLIVER NORTH

Contents

Acknowledgments

First, my sincere thanks to the Soldiers, Sailors, Airmen, Guardsmen, and Marines with whom I have kept company throughout this long war. The young Americans I have been covering for FOX News since September 11, 2001, forfeited the comforts of home, absented themselves from the affection of loved ones, and volunteered to go into harm's way in some of the most difficult and dangerous places on earth. They are the best and bravest of their generation. We are all better for their service.

Heroes are people who place themselves at risk for the benefit of others. That certainly describes the audacious volunteers who wear our nation's uniform in this long fight—and their families here at home. I'm especially indebted to—and inspired by—those who have endured the loss of loved ones and the resilience of the heroes who have lost limbs and yet persevere through terrible trauma. Their triumph over tragedy is the heart and soul of this book, and I'm thankful they have allowed us to tell their stories.

My gratitude to FOX News chairman Roger Ailes and his leadership team: Bill Shine, Michael Clemente, John Stack, and Pamela Browne. Since the beginning of this long war they have made it possible for our small combat coverage group to "embed" with more than fifty U.S. and allied military units and capture stunning imagery for broadcast on FOX News Channel and use in this and our other American Heroes books.

Mal James, Christian Galdabini, Chris Jackson, Chuck Holton, Greg Johnson, Martin Hinton, Steve Tierney, and Andy Stenner—my camera-

FOX News Team in Afghanistan. *FOX News*

men and field producers—braved enemy fire, improvised explosive devices, suicide bombers, and countless long days and sleepless nights in difficult and dangerous places to capture dramatic images so we could document America's heroes on distant and dangerous battlefields.

This work would never have been published were it not for the attentiveness of my counselors and friends Robert Barnett and Michael O'Connor at Williams & Connolly. Their relationships with FOX News general counsel Dianne Brandi and Threshold Editions president and publisher Louise Burke made this work a reality.

As with every other book I have completed during more than two decades, Marsha Fishbaugh and her husband, Dave—a Vietnam War veteran and U.S. Army helicopter pilot—have somehow made it possible for me to get to where I needed to be—on time! And once again, Duane Ward and his team at Premiere have agreed to promote and market this work so that Americans from every walk of life will get to know the heroes in these pages.

At Threshold Editions imprint at Simon & Schuster, vice president and senior editor Mitchell Ivers, editorial assistant Natasha Simons, art director Lisa Litwack, production editor Al Madocs, and publicity director Jennifer Robinson have ensured that the eyewitness accounts and imagery in this work will be preserved to inspire others for generations to come.

Tom Kilgannon, president of Freedom Alliance, and the team he leads are a major inspiration for this book. Calvin Coolidge, Pepper Ailor, Tim Strickler, and Alicia Behm have provided extraordinary, generous support to Gold Star Families, the sons and daughters of our fallen, and real help to our severely wounded since this fight started. The relationships Freedom Alliance forged with military and veterans hospitals, the Marine Corps' Wounded Warrior Regiment, and

Oliver North and Bob Hamer with American Heroes at the 2012 Army-Navy Game. *Freedom Alliance*

others who care for our casualties have been crucial to thousands of troops and their loved ones. A brief description of how Freedom Alliance helps and honors America's Heroes is on pages 253–54.

My friend and collaborator in this work, former Marine officer and undercover FBI Special Agent Bob Hamer, shares my faith, friendships, and admiration for those who overcome terrible adversity with courage and love. His compassion and respect for young Americans who demonstrate these qualities are coupled with a gift for being able to eloquently tell their stories. Bob has spent days, weeks, and months with the families front and center in this book—and countless others besides. It has been a joy to work with him on this project.

Most important, the woman to whom this book is dedicated has repeatedly picked up the responsibilities of bill payer, household manager, lone protector of four children, and now, grandparent to fourteen while I have been off on lengthy trips to faraway places. She knows the uncertainty of a waiting spouse while her mate is off at war—and what it's like to pray a delegation headed by a chaplain never comes to the front door delivering a message of terrible loss. As it was when I was on active duty, Betsy is still my best friend, wisest counselor, and greatest encouragement for keeping company with heroes.

Semper Fidelis,

Oliver North
Camp Leatherneck
Helmand Province, Afghanistan
10 July 2013

their foxholes. Estab
ce, this bond will always endu

Introduction

WALTER REED NATIONAL MILITARY MEDICAL CENTER
BETHESDA, MARYLAND
4 JULY 2013

The first U.S. military casualties inflicted by radical Islamic terrorists on September 11, 2001, didn't make it to this hospital. All 106 living victims, injured and burned inside the Pentagon when American Airlines Flight 77 was hijacked and smashed into the west wall of the building, were treated at other medical facilities. In the days since, however, this hospital and its predecessor namesake have treated more than thirty-five thousand wounded Soldiers, Sailors, Airmen, Guardsmen, and Marines.

Many of the grievously injured young Americans cared for in this hospital—and others like it—would not have survived in earlier wars. Thanks to advances in battlefield trauma treatment, rapid helicopter medical evacuation, forward field hospitals, advanced surgical procedures, and antibiotics, thousands of those who would otherwise have perished are alive today.

For most of those wounded on the battlefield, their initial medical treatment was provided by a field medic or a Navy medical corpsman. A sculpture at the main entrance to the hospital called *The Unspoken Bond* is a tribute to these "First Responders of the Battlefield."

The statue, a Navy corpsman dragging a wounded Marine to safety, is inscribed: "This memorial is dedicated to the hospital corpsmen who served with the Marines in the Pacific during World War II. 'Doc' was that special comrade who pulled them to safety, patched their wounds and shared their foxholes. Established in war and ennobled in peace, this bond shall always endure." That same sentiment applies in every armed conflict—whether it's an Army medic, an Air Force "P.J.," or a Navy corpsman risking life and limb to save another.

Standing before this sculpture with Jack Fowler, the Navy corpsman who bound up my wounds during a bloody battle in Vietnam, I am once again reminded what selfless service really

Facing page: Oliver North and "Doc" Jack Fowler at Peter Wilde's *The Unspoken Bond.* Freedom Alliance

is. Amazingly, "Doc" Fowler is still treating wounded Marines—and Sailors, Soldiers, Guardsmen, and Airmen.

In 1969, after he was wounded in action, Jack came home, went to college on the GI Bill, and returned to service as an officer. During a thirty-three-year career in Navy medicine, he has treated thousands for traumatic brain injury, chronic pain, and post-traumatic stress. Some of his patients are in this book.

Each time I return from an overseas assignment for FOX News, I come to this place to visit the troops who were wounded during our "embed" with their units. Doc Fowler has accompanied me through the corridors of this hospital and into the rooms of shattered survivors more times than I can remember. The care and compassion for the heroes recovering here—and for their loved ones praying for healing—are evident in every visit. So too are the remarkable advances in military medical care since we were wounded in Vietnam.

Jack's vivid description is graphic—but important to understanding how things have changed:

> In our war, a field corpsman had a Unit One with basic first-aid equipment, a few glass bottles of Ringers saline solution, battle dressings and tourniquets, morphine syrettes, patches to cover a sucking chest wound, an emergency "trache tube" to open an airway, some sterile scalpels, suture sets, scissors, tweezers, hemostats, some copper sulfate pads for burns, and not much more. Most of our casualties were fragment wounds from shrapnel and bullet holes. A badly wounded Marine with arterial bleeding in Northern I Corps might make it if we could get a helo in immediately to lift him out to the "Delta-Med" field hospital at Dong Ha or maybe out to a hospital ship, but in bad weather that didn't always happen. And even when we did get 'em out—it was usually many days before the wounded got home. Today, almost everything is different.
>
> There are still some things that are the same as it was back then: it still takes just an instant to get terribly wounded; but in this war, most of the casualties are from improvised explosive devices (IEDs). Many of the most seriously injured have severed or mangled limbs, severe arterial hemorrhaging, and traumatic brain injuries that may or may not be immediately evident. The good news is that today's field corpsmen and medics are better trained and equipped than we were.
>
> In addition to modern versions of the first-aid gear I carried, they also have blood volume expanders in plastic pouches for treating shock and blood loss, hemostatic

> (clotting) material, even battle dressings impregnated with hemostatic gauze to stop bleeding.
>
> Best of all, most of our wounded are rapidly moved—usually in minutes rather than hours—by helicopter to the best trauma care in the world at a field hospital in-theater. When they are stabilized, they're put aboard a U.S. Air Force C-17 "Nightingale"—a flying hospital—and flown to Landstuhl Regional Medical Center in Germany. Then—usually within seventy-two to ninety-six hours after being wounded—they arrive at Andrews Air Force Base and are brought here.
>
> This is where the high-speed trip stops. Despite all our advances in medicine, recuperation and rehabilitation still take much longer than it did to get hurt. Many of our casualties need multiple surgeries. And while most of them are remarkably fit when they were wounded, healing for body, mind, and spirit is nearly always more painful than the original injury. Recovery also requires the active participation of those who love them—their parents, spouses, children, siblings, and close friends.

In the dozen years since Operation Enduring Freedom began in Afghanistan, the U.S. military has transformed how families can stay connected with their wounded Soldiers, Sailors, Airmen, Guardsmen, and Marines. During previous wars there were no provisions for bringing family members to a military hospital where their wounded loved ones were recuperating. If they wanted to do so, they had to get there on their own. That's no longer the case.

Each service now has programs for notifying, maintaining contact with, and helping get immediate family members to the bedsides of our casualties. For example, the Marine Corps' Wounded Warrior Regiment, headquartered at Quantico, Virginia, now has detachments at military hospitals like Walter Reed NMMC. Part of their task is to facilitate travel and lodging for spouses or parents so they can join their wounded mates or offspring.

It's a morale-building program that has now been replicated in every branch of the U.S. armed forces. While it isn't perfect—nothing in war ever is—it works. Best of all, support for the families of our wounded is now a mission for every senior military leader in this war. Much of that is the result of "lessons learned" in this long fight.

In March and April 2003, during the first phase of Operation Iraqi Freedom, our two-man FOX News team was embedded with elements of Marine Regimental Combat Team 5 (RCT 5)—a 6,500-strong Air-Ground Task Force, leading the eastern attack north from Kuwait to Baghdad. Griff Jenkins and I rode on dozens of emergency casualty evacuation (cas-evac)

FOX News cameraman Griff Jenkins glad to be alive after another harrowing cas-evac mission aboard a Marine CH-46 helo during the fight for Baghdad in 2003. *FOX News*

flights aboard the CH-46 helicopters of HMM-268—the "Red Dragons"—commanded by Lieutenant Colonel Jerry Driscoll.

An excerpt from a report we filed on April 5, after a particularly hair-raising cas-evac mission in Al Aziziyah—just south of Saddam's capital:

> Somehow, Driscoll manages to put the CH-46 down in the middle of an intersection. . . . Marines, dismounted from their vehicles, are firing into the buildings in every direction. An M-1 tank's main gun booms above the din. . . . Marines and Corpsmen carrying litters start running in a low crouch for the back of our helicopter. As the casualties are being loaded aboard, an RPG passes in front of the helicopter, exploding in the dirt about fifteen meters beyond us, prompting Driscoll to call over the radio, "How much longer, folks? This is a pretty sporty zone."
>
> While I'm considering this description of the hottest LZ I've ever been in, three Humvees race up from the left, machine guns blazing from their rooftop turrets. It's the mobile command post for "Grizzly Six," Colonel Joe Dunford, the commanding officer of RCT-5.
>
> With the enemy pinned down by heavy fire from the Humvees, eleven casualties aboard our helicopter and ten on the bird behind us, the two heavily loaded CH-46s lift a few feet off the ground. With power lines just inches away from the blade tips, they rotate 180 degrees so they can head out over "friendlies."

Though we never broadcast the faces of American casualties, a FOX News viewer watching at home thought she recognized her son among the wounded Marines aboard my helicopter. The inquiry from an anxious Marine's mother was relayed to us, but we didn't know—and there was no way to find out.

That's unlikely to occur today because senior military officers in every service have made next-of-kin notification, casualty tracking, and family support a primary mission in every branch of our armed forces. One of those who helped make these issues a priority in the Marines is "Grizzly Six"—the RCT commander who courageously raced into that 2003 gunfight to protect his wounded Marines. He now wears four stars.

In February 2013, after serving two years as Assistant Commandant of the Marine Corps, "Fighting Joe" Dunford was appointed by the president and confirmed by the Senate as Commander of the NATO International Security Assistance Force (ISAF) and U.S. Forces

With "Grizzly Six," now a four-star in Afghanistan, July 2013. *FOX News*

Afghanistan. Joe Dunford's rapid promotions have not dimmed his concern for America's "hurt heroes" and their families. His wife, Ellyn, is cut from the same bolt of cloth.

★ ★ ★

The profession of arms in the United States armed forces has to be the most challenging vocation in the world—for those who serve, and for those who love the service member. There is no other calling I know of that places so many challenges on familial relationships, so much stress on loved ones, as military service. I didn't always grasp that.

In 2005 the Marine Corps permitted our FOX News team to do a "double embed." Part of our *War Stories* team went with me to Ramadi, Iraq—then the bloodiest place on the planet—with 1st Battalion, 6th Marines. While we were in Anbar Province, senior producer Greg Johnson, a camera crew, and a satellite team went to Camp Lejeune, North Carolina, the unit's home base.

The "rules of engagement" for our documentary teams were very simple: we agreed not to broadcast the names of anyone without permission of the deployed Marines *and* their families. And we made a commitment to not display home addresses, show license plates, or put children on TV without both parents' agreement.

Titled "From the Frontlines to the Homefront," it was an emotion-packed broadcast, for the Marines, their families—and for me. Weeks later, when I returned home, Betsy said: "That was a great episode of *War Stories.* I'm glad you finally understand what we all went through while you were off at your wars. . . ."

A Marine contingent departing for Afghanistan. *DOD*

Some of the toughest moments for service members and their families are days when they depart on deployment to war. There are almost always tears. *DOD*

Oliver North with Lieutenant Colonel Bill Jurney in Ramadi, Iraq. *FOX News*

While Bill and his battalion were in the bloodiest place on the planet, Sue Jurney held things together on the home front at Camp Lejeune, North Carolina. *FOX News*

She wasn't being mean-spirited or acrimonious—just stating the obvious. Parting at the beginning of a deployment is never easy. There are almost always tears. When small children are involved there are always questions: "Why is my daddy [or my mommy] leaving?" And of course, "Will he [or she] ever come home?"

Lieutenant Colonel Bill Jurney, the commanding officer of 1st Battalion, 6th Marines, described what he missed during these separations this way: "It's the simple things. Seeing your kids asleep when they don't know you are there. . . . Coming home and playing in the front yard with all the neighborhood kids. Those are the things I miss the most."

From my experience, he's spot-on. But it's also true that when a service member deploys to a war zone they are surrounded by comrades focused on the mission at hand, shared hardships, adrenaline, and often a singular aim of staying alive. For those left at home there is loneliness, uncertainty, anxiety, and the sole responsibility of raising a family.

Bill Jurney again: "We're not asking anybody to feel sorry for us. . . . Most spouses of United States Marines are pretty dog-gone strong-willed and independent. They have learned to adapt and live their lives and raise our families in our absence."

His wife, Sue, agrees: "It's not just a job, it's a lifestyle, and it affects everybody in your family. Military spouses sacrifice every day. The way we handle things at home is important. . . . If our guys over there are concerned and worried about how things are going at home, they can't stay focused on their mission. . . ."

That's a unique perspective in today's culture. Few relationships in our society are stress-tested like those in military families. That's why "Fighting Joe" Dunford describes his wife, Ellyn, as "the most valuable player in the Dunford family."

Just two days before her husband flew off to take command of U.S. forces in Afghanistan, Ellyn Dunford agreed to sit down with our FOX News team at their new quarters on a military base near Washington. She shrugs off Joe's "MVP" characterization with a grin—but she also says with a knowing laugh, "Having two little kids in diapers is hard" no matter where you live or what your husband does.

They have been married since 1984. Yet, without the need to consult a calendar, Ellyn estimates she and her husband have spent more than a third of their marriage separated by Joe's overseas deployments and the cumulative weeks and months he spent in the field on training exercises and military schools. She acknowledges that constant moves as "Military Migrant Workers" make it challenging to raise three children and build her practice as a physical therapist. But she smiles when she says, "Our oldest son went to eleven different schools by the time he graduated from high school."

With Ellyn Dunford, wife of General "Fighting Joe" Dunford, the day before he deployed as Senior American Commander in Afghanistan. *FOX News*

It's not a complaint—just a fact of life. With justifiable pride she shows us around the house she occupied only three days earlier and says, "We've moved four times in the last six years. I've learned to pack light—and quickly."

When asked if she worried when she saw news reports about her husband in combat, Ellyn pauses a moment before responding: "Like most military wives with a deployed spouse, I watched the news. We all spoke with those who came back from deployment about what was going on, and some of his troops were very free in what they told me. . . . I tried not to think about it that much. I equate it to being married to a fireman. You know he's going out on calls, and you know there's great danger, but you don't dwell on it."

Multiple moves, combat deployments, and lengthy separations haven't dimmed Ellyn Dunford's affection for her Marine. Asked to reflect on his best qualities, she said, "I admire the way my husband has been faithful . . . to the Marine Corps and our country . . . to those he serves with . . . and as a father and a husband. Everyone struggles with juggling the different aspects of life. . . . I think our family has done it pretty well."

Ellyn Dunford's family clearly comes first. But her commitment to the families of those who serve with her husband is a close second. When Joe commanded RCT-5 in combat she spent thirty to fifty hours per week maintaining contact with the families of those he led. She describes that period of her life in a single word: "intense."

"I shared my email address with every single spouse within the headquarters group, and then with all the battalion commanders' spouses. . . . I told them to forward to me any issues they couldn't deal with . . . 'send them up to me, and I'll take care of it.' . . . I went to every memorial service and funeral in the Camp Pendleton area that I found out about."

She still makes countless visits to military hospitals to meet with wounded Marines and their families. Using the words of a military wife, a mother, and a health-care professional, she knows how crucial families and loved ones are for healing and rehabilitation and why such hospital visits make a difference:

"It's knowing somebody cared . . . that they came, not just for a photo op or because it's on a checklist of things to be done this week. . . . For them to know that you actually care is very important because their service member's injury is the great unknown. They don't know how they're going to heal. . . . What's going to happen after they leave the hospital? Having a visit from a senior person who responds to their concerns is reassuring."

Ellyn Dunford is well aware that being the wife of America's senior battlefield commander puts her under a microscope. She describes her new role as "part health-care professional," part "mentor to others," and part "educator . . . in a positive way" to help Americans understand the real needs of our warriors and their families.

She points out that today just "one percent of our population serves" in our military, so few of our fellow citizens even know a military family. For many civilians "their context may be a movie. But there are very few movies I've seen that reflect my experience or my husband's."

Ellyn has been asked, "Will you be going to Afghanistan with your husband?" Others have inquired if she is compensated for the time she spends visiting hospitals and counseling spouses on employment opportunities. Her answer: "I was paid back with the appreciation of the people I helped. . . ."

I ask her what she wants the American people to know about the young people serving today. Her response is particularly relevant to the stories in this book:

"Don't patronize them. . . . Don't be afraid of them. . . . Don't pity them. Treat them as individuals—human beings of great value. You can't paint military families with a broad brush. Each situation is going to be a little bit different. . . .

". . . All of them are affected just as much as a civilian family by our economic situation. . . . For those who have been badly injured, rehabilitation is the most immediate concern. . . . For other members and their spouses it's the transition out of the service and finding good employment. . . . Some will need additional training and education to be productive. . . . They volunteered to go into harm's way to protect us. . . . When they leave the service, they deserve to have good jobs. . . . That's the best way we can honor them and their families for their selfless sacrifice."

At the end of our interview, I ask Ellyn Dunford what she would tell her grandchildren when they asked what she did during this long war. Her response: "I'm going to say, 'I took care of my family and other people's families.'"

That sounds just right to those whose stories follow.

Brian Meyer on a typical combat patrol, ready for anything. *Brian Meyer*

1

TWO FINGERS TO HOLD

Jesseca and Brian Meyer

The radio in the Combat Operations Center (COC) crackled with a garbled message followed by the nine-line EOD order. The Marine watch officer monitoring the communication traffic shouted through the hole in the primitive mud wall, alerting Staff Sergeant Brian Meyer and members of his Explosive Ordnance Disposal (EOD) team. A suspected improvised explosive device, commonly known as an IED, had been discovered by a squad of Marines on routine patrol and now an EOD response team was needed somewhere outside the wire of Patrol Base Almas.

In the sixth month of his seven-month combat deployment to Afghanistan, Brian had made about eighty such trips beyond the confines of PB Almas to dispose of IEDs, the terrorists' weapon of choice. He didn't know at the time that this would be his last trip and his longest journey.

* * *

Her radiant smile and stunning features captivate you immediately. Even though she is just five feet one, her father's Aztec blood and her mother's Spanish heritage make Jesseca Meyer stand out in any crowd.

They met in August 2008 at the Democratic National Convention in Denver. Jesseca, a college junior majoring in sports management, was working at the Pepsi Center as a security supervisor and was assigned to accompany a Marine Corps bomb team tasked with sweeping the third level of the arena for any explosive devices. Four Marines paraded in with their equipment and their egos. Brian, a member of the team, was immediately drawn to her beauty. He sensed she'd spent a lifetime around tough guys, so he decided to turn on the charm rather than the testosterone. His efforts paid off and before the convention ended a friendship was formed as she stayed in Denver and he returned to Camp Pendleton, north of San Diego. The relationship progressed as the couple talked by phone daily and texted in between calls.

A few months later, Brian asked Jesseca to come to San Diego for a Halloween celebration at his house. At the time, Brian and three other Marines, Justin Schmalstieg, Bryan Carter, and Mark Wojciechowski, known to his friends as Tony Wojo, all assigned to 1st EOD Company, rented a home outside Camp Pendleton's back gate. As Jesseca would learn, life in the Marine Corps is fragile. All four roommates would go on to earn Purple Hearts; two would die in combat. Just six months after the party on April 30, 2009, twenty-five-year-old Staff Sergeant Mark Wojciechowski was killed in action in Al Anbar Province, Iraq, three months into his second combat deployment.

Brian and Jesseca's friendship grew into love. The first week of May 2010, they flew to Florida for the annual EOD Memorial Ball, an event honoring members of their brotherhood who made the ultimate sacrifice.

During one of the presentations, a ranking member of the EOD community praised the wives for the extraordinary role they played in supporting their husbands while doing some of the most

Pepsi Center in Denver, Colorado, where Jesseca and Brian first met in 2008. *Chamber of Commerce*

Top: Justin Schmalstieg, Bryan Carter, and Brian Meyer before deploying overseas. *Bryan Carter*
Bottom: Brian Meyer and Mark Wojciechowski in their dress blues. *Bryan Carter*

EOD Memorial, Niceville, Florida. *Bryan Carter*

dangerous work in the military. As thoughts flashed through her mind about what Brian and his men did on each and every assignment, Jesseca knew she wanted to be that support and spend the rest of her life with him.

Maybe sensing Jesseca's commitment, the next day, as they walked along Florida's Emerald Coast, the macho Marine stopped, got down on one knee, and asked her to marry him. She eyed the handsome Marine with an adoring sense of humor but no ring and replied, "Is this a joke?" When he convinced her he was serious, she agreed.

☆ ☆ ☆

Rather than continuing to pay rent, Brian and fellow EOD Marine Bryan Carter purchased a home outside Camp Pendleton's back gate, and it became their shared residence. To offset the costs of the mortgage they rented two of the bedrooms to other Marines.

This was now home for Brian and Jesseca, who were married in a private ceremony at a Las Vegas wedding chapel on May 29, 2010, four weeks after he proposed and just months before he deployed to Afghanistan.

Between the wedding and his departure in October, Brian spent more than half his time away from home in pre-deployment work-ups and training.

What little time they did spend together was often in the company of other EOD Marines and their wives. Jesseca met the wives and girlfriends of Brian's friends, who welcomed her into the fellowship of EOD warriors. Although the Marines could laugh off the inherent dangers in the job, she was scared and the feelings never subsided. She took comfort in knowing he was skilled at his job, but still, the unknown was always lurking. One misstep meant instant carnage.

While some wives packed up and went home when their husbands deployed, returning at the end of the deployment, Jesseca stayed in Oceanside. All of her family was in Colorado, but being in the company of wives with husbands overseas or who had recently returned from a deployment seemed the right move. She knew Brian's assignment in a combat zone would bring on a flood of emotions that might not be understood by those at home. With the exception of Heidi Wilson and Aaron Root and his wife, Leslie, all her friends were in the Marine Corps or married to Marines. They understood the special toll a deployment took on a relationship. Staying in Oceanside meant each could carry the others' burdens; burdens so few in the country were carrying.

☆ ☆ ☆

Brian and Jesseca at the EOD Memorial Ball the day before he proposed. *Brian Meyer*

Moments after being announced as husband and wife. *Brian Meyer*

Brian and Jesseca savoring the last few moments before deployment. *Brian Meyer*

How Brian and his EOD team dispose of captured explosives. *Brian Meyer*

Brian's third combat deployment began in October 2010 as part of the continuing commitment to Operation Enduring Freedom, the war in Afghanistan.

He and Sergeant Bobby Conlon formed their two-man team at Pendleton and were surprised when they arrived at Camp Leatherneck in Afghanistan's Helmand Province to have a third Marine, Sergeant Eric Lunson, assigned to the team. The men spent a week at Leatherneck taking mandatory classes on the law of war, checking equipment, and waiting for spaces to open up at the forward operating bases or patrol bases. Unlike the typical Marine Corps combat unit, which trains and fights as one, the EOD teams were augmented or "farmed out" to the various infantry commands, functioning in a firefighter's role responding from crisis to crisis as the calls c ame in.

Initially the three-man team was attached to a weapons company at Sangin, Afghanistan. The work was sporadic yet always dangerous.

On a day in November, his team rendered eight IEDs safe within an hour and then in December, while responding to an IED call out, EOD teammate Bobby Conlon was shot through the arm and Brian was hit in the back. Fortunately for Brian, he was wearing his ballistic vest with the SAPI plate in place. The Small Arms Protective Insert (SAPI), a ceramic plate strategically located in pockets on the vest, saved Brian from almost certain death. The plate was damaged but Brian lived.

Shortly after this event, on December 15, one of Brian's best friends and former housemates, Staff Sergeant Justin Schmalstieg, was killed while working with a Marine recon unit in the northern part of the province. Justin was posthumously promoted to gunnery sergeant, but the promotion did little to lessen the pain of the death of a close friend and colleague.

The SAPI plate that saved Brian Meyer's life. *Brian Meyer*

In late December, Gunnery Sergeant John Hayes, the team leader at Patrol Base Almas, was critically wounded. Hayes had defused one IED and as he moved toward a second stepped on an undetected device. John lost both legs and suffered extensive internal damage. Brian was reassigned to

Sergeant Bobby Conlon and Sergeant Eric Lunson preparing to dispose of an antitank missile and other explosives. *Brian Meyer*

Brian's EOD team along with members of the Afghan National Army after dismantling eight IEDs in an hour.
Brian Meyer.

Sergeant Bobby Conlon after being wounded. *Brian Meyer*

Staff Sergeant Bryan Carter, Staff Sergeant Brian Meyer, and Gunnery Sergeant Jeb Adle at Camp Leatherneck in December 2010. *Bryan Carter*

Staff Sergeant Bryan Carter and Sergeant Jarret Garibaldi holding Old Glory over two hundred pounds of explosives discovered during an operation. *Bryan Carter*

Staff Sergeant Bryan Carter dismantling an IED discovered while on patrol near Safar, Afghanistan. *Jarret Garibaldi*

Staff Sergeant Bryan Carter carried these dismantled IEDs in his backpack so they could be analyzed back at the FOB. *Bryan Carter*

replace Gunny Hayes. He and Eric Lunson headed to PB Almas, fifteen minutes down the road from the forward operating base at Sangin. At Almas they teamed up with Sergeant Charlie Linville, who had worked with Gunnery Sergeant Hayes.

Within three weeks of Brian assuming team leader responsibilities at PB Almas, Charlie Linville stepped on an IED and was medically evacuated.

Sergeant Sean Honsberger replaced Charlie. Throughout the deployment, the EOD teams in Helmand Province were in a constant state of transition as the technically trained Marines replaced their wounded colleagues.

* * *

On March 14, 2011, Brian once again welcomed the opportunity to do the job he was trained to do.

It didn't take a verbal order from Meyer, a ten-year veteran of the Marine Corps, to assemble the men on this bright sunny afternoon. Sergeants Sean Honsberger and Eric Lunson knew their mission and quickly gathered their gear.

Although various thoughts flooded their minds as they prepared to venture beyond the confines of the patrol base, the men patiently awaited an abbreviated team of Marines to return to the remote compound and then accompany the EOD techs to the discovery site. There was some nervous chatter but not much. Though never routine, EOD techs, risking it all with each assignment, took life as it came, often employing gallows humor as they stared death in the face . . . and laughed. They typically wanted to get "before"—with limbs—and "after"—without limbs—pictures and promised each other that if they were blown up a teammate would snap a photo at the site of the detonation.

Considering the advanced technology of the tools of war, the EOD kit Brian Meyer carried to dispose of land mines was pretty simple . . . a seat belt cutter, a clamp, 120 feet of half-inch tubular nylon rope, and a hook. The bomb suits and robots of Hollywood's *Hurt Locker* worked but when outfitted in one you had about fifteen minutes before you became a heatstroke casualty. As with nearly every call Brian and his team received on this deployment, they would have to walk miles in terrain accessible only by foot before they arrived at the site. Not only was it impracticable to make such a hike in a bomb suit; any remote-controlled devices had to be transported by truck, and trucks couldn't navigate the rugged territory or the soft furrowed farmland.

Patrol Base Almas was in Helmand Province near Sangin, a town of approximately fifteen thousand people, located near the Kajaki hydroelectric dam on the Helmand River.

Sergeant Jarret Garibaldi holding a Holly Stick talking with local children in Durzay, Afghanistan. *Bryan Carter*

These EOD suits popularized by Hollywood are impossible to wear in the rugged terrain of Afghanistan. *DOD*

ISAF forces at Kajaki Dam. *ISAF OR-6 Mitch Moore*

Building a "HESCO house" in the Afghan desert. *DOD*

The dam and its attendant irrigation system made this otherwise barren desert lush farmland. The Marines assumed responsibility for the area in October 2010, taking over from the British, who had manned the area the four previous years.

Patrol Base Almas was short on comforts and long on danger. There were no showers or mess halls. The men ate MREs (Meal, Ready-to-Eat), individual, self-contained food rations consisting of 1,200-calorie meals, or UGRs (Unitized Group Rations), a tray-based heat-and-serve entrée warmed by immersing the tray in a hot-water module. Neither came close to home cooking. The only "modern convenience" was a Hesco-constructed latrine with a tube in which to urinate and military-issued double-bag waste disposal kits called Wag Bags, accompanied by toilet paper, hand sanitizer, and nontoxic Poo powder for breaking down solid waste. Electricity at the patrol base came by way of a temperamental generator and all the water was bottled.

Approximately twenty Marines called the patrol base home for their seven-month deployment. The base was in reality a residential compound consisting of primitive buildings made of mud and stucco. Roughly the size of two football fields, the compound was surrounded by concertina wire, providing limited defense.

Like the rest of the facilities, the windowless EOD room was primitive and makeshift. What doubled as the living quarters and the team's operational center had a cement floor and thick mud walls. The Marines pounded nails in the dirt bulkheads to hang gear, with a few maps of the area providing most of the decorations.

* * *

Back in Oceanside, the home that seemed like a subdued frat house was almost lonely. Co-owners Brian Meyer and Bryan Carter were both part of the October deployment. Jesseca stayed, as did Bryan's fiancée, Amanda. Housemate Staff Sergeant Parker Blanche, another EOD Marine, remained behind for this deployment, preparing for his next one.

The other military wives were supportive and set up AMD parties . . . Another Month Down. On the tenth of every month the wives would gather and celebrate another month closer to their husbands coming home. For too many in the group, the husbands came home early, catastrophically injured, or in the case of one close friend, dead.

Anxiety shrouded every waking moment. Early in the deployment Jesseca missed a call from Brian and cried for an hour, ruining her day and leading her to vow, "I'll never miss another call." Her cell phone became a constant companion.

The days and months ran together. A typical day for her consisted of a workout to relieve the stress and then work at 24 Hour Fitness, a gym in Oceanside. Sundays meant church and usually a shift at the gym. Communications were limited with Brian because of his remote location. Emails were infrequent and phone calls were limited to one or two a month. It was an emotional roller coaster.

* * *

Throughout the deployment, the Marines from all units suffered major casualties. The British suffered a third of all their Afghan war casualties in Sangin, and for the Marines who assumed responsibility for taming the province, little changed. Patrol units came under constant small arms fire and were subjected to the ever-present improvised explosive devices.

The EOD tech's responsibility was more than just disposing of the device with a controlled detonation. The pre- and post-blast analysis was important in identifying trends, bomb-making facilities, or the bomb makers themselves. In essence, Brian and the EOD technicians were playing *CSI: Afghanistan,* only there were no retakes. Missed marks and botched lines in this real-life drama had life-and-death consequences.

It was a team of five or six Marines who returned to the patrol base on the afternoon of March 14. Although no patrol was routine, the trek back to the location of the suspected IED was uneventful. The growing season was just beginning and the farmers were returning to farm the countryside. The patrol encountered few locals and what farmers there were in the area avoided the Marines. The men slushed their way through the less traveled shallow irrigation ditches rather than walking the sunbaked dirt paths bordering either side of the canals, the more likely spot to hide an improvised explosive device.

It took about an hour winding their way through farmland, canals, and ditches before they arrived at the site. Brian was quickly briefed on the situation. A local national pointed out to one of the patrol members a possible IED on a dirt path connecting two compounds. When a Marine combat engineer approached the site and scanned the location with a metal detector, it popped positive, so the Marines quickly backed off, set up a security perimeter, and called in the specialists.

Brian and his team took a visual of the situation before Brian commenced an indirect route toward the suspected device. The tension was high as he feared not only the device detonating but any secondary devices also exploding.

He set up a safe area and began the dangerous and tedious procedure of dismantling an improvised explosive device. The IED was planted in an anthill, thus disguising the recently

Marines traversing a canal in Helmand Province. *USMC Sgt. Jacob Harrer*

Hooking a pull rope to a buried IED is one of the most dangerous moments in the life of an EOD tech.

USMC Sgt. Logan Pierce

disturbed ground. Marines on patrol knew enough not to step on a loose pile of dirt, but few would suspect an IED planted in an anthill and might chance stepping on the mound of earth.

Now combatting ants, crawling over his hands and arms, Brian quickly discovered the device and carefully separated the components, identifying the power supply and pressure plate. Even with the experience of defusing hundreds of devices, the uncertainty of death remained. It wasn't just a game of hide-and-seek with the enemy. This was life-and-death for Brian Meyer and the Marines in the immediate area. Fear lurked in the back of his mind but rather than block out the emotion, he played to it. Fear brought focus.

With the component parts severed, Brian carefully hooked a rope to the main charge, a three-liter plastic jug used by the locals to store cooking oil. This bottle, however, was filled with ammonium nitrate and aluminum powder. With the rope secured to the jug, Brian followed a metal-swept path back to the perimeter patrol.

The men assumed they were safe from a possible detonation, despite the EOD axiom "If you can see an IED, it can see you." The Marines tensed and sought cover as Brian gave the rope a slow, steady pull until taut. Shouting "fire in the hole," he offered a strong tug, assuming that would detonate the main charge . . . nothing. He tried a second time with an equally strong jerk . . . still nothing. Waiting what he hoped was a lifetime in case there was a time-delayed fuse, the Marine moved forward, taking "the longest walk," as EOD technicians call the approach to an explosive device. The jug was still in the hole and he assumed it fell back into the cavity after being yanked hard twice. He carefully bent over the main charge, grabbed it, and learned too late it had an anti-tampering mechanism . . . the device exploded in his hand!

The sound was deafening and a bright blast of orange and crimson flames shot forth like an erupting volcano. Reflecting the calm demeanor he displayed throughout his career, Brian's first thought was "Oops!" as the earth below him shook. He was blown into the air, landing facedown. As he faded in and out of consciousness, he lacked the strength to assess himself. His memories of that day are dulled by the shock his body was experiencing, but the Marines reacted quickly as the Navy corpsman administered lifesaving first aid. Brian recalls seeing his hands wrapped in tourniquets and his ears ringing, muddling most of the conversation. After catching a glimpse of his good leg, he assumed the injuries might not be that bad and made a few weak attempts at humor. He tried to remain awake and ward off shock by singing off-key the Bee Gees' hit single "Stayin' Alive," and provided an anemic smile as Eric Lunson snapped a picture, keeping a promise the EOD Marines made to each other.

* * *

This photo was taken by Sergeant Eric "Lundobomber" Lunson as a Navy corpsman and Sergeant Sean Honsberger administer immediate aid to Brian. *Eric Lunson*

Jesseca had emailed Brian the day before, reminding him how much she loved him and adding, "Please, please be careful."

Amanda, Bryan Carter's fiancée, was an *Army Wives* fan and soon Jesseca was hooked on the TV drama, too. When she got home late that evening after working a full shift at the gym an episode was airing. Jesseca plopped down on the couch, hoping to relax before heading to bed. Most of the episodes were dramatic but this one had a singular emotional appeal. It ended with the wives holding hands as a black SUV pulled to the curb and two uniformed men exited the vehicle. Jesseca's heart ached as she pictured one of her best friends, Ann Schmalstieg. Ann's husband, Justin, died a few months earlier and Jesseca could only imagine what emotions ran through Ann's soul as she received the notification.

An accomplished artist and fitness instructor, Ann was shy and private but those qualities resonated with Jesseca. Justin and Ann, friends since high school, married thirteen months before he was killed. The son of two Pittsburgh police detectives, he had been in the Marine Corps nine years with multiple combat deployments. It was easy to see why Jesseca and Brian gravitated to the couple. Justin was quiet and calm, two qualities that make a good EOD technician but don't always match the preconceived notions of self-assured Marines. Like Brian, Justin was mission-focused with a strong sense of duty. On December 15, he was heading back to camp following a nighttime patrol. Justin's mission was to clear a path for the Marine recon unit he was assisting. Defusing an IED in daylight was dangerous enough, but on this night, darkness won and another Marine was sacrificed on freedom's altar.

When the episode ended, Jesseca headed for bed. A phone call the next day changed her life forever.

⁂

Once they got Brian on a helicopter the corpsman gave him something and he was out, waking up at the Heath N. Craig Joint Theater Hospital at Bagram Air Base in the Parwan Province of Afghanistan.

He was heavily medicated but could tell by the bandages the injuries were massive. Three combat deployments had exposed him to the death and destruction of war. Many friends died and many lost limbs; death didn't scare him, mutilation did. His constant prayer was "God, don't take the hands. Legs are overrated but let me keep my hands." Looking down at the thick gauze he was afraid both hands were gone.

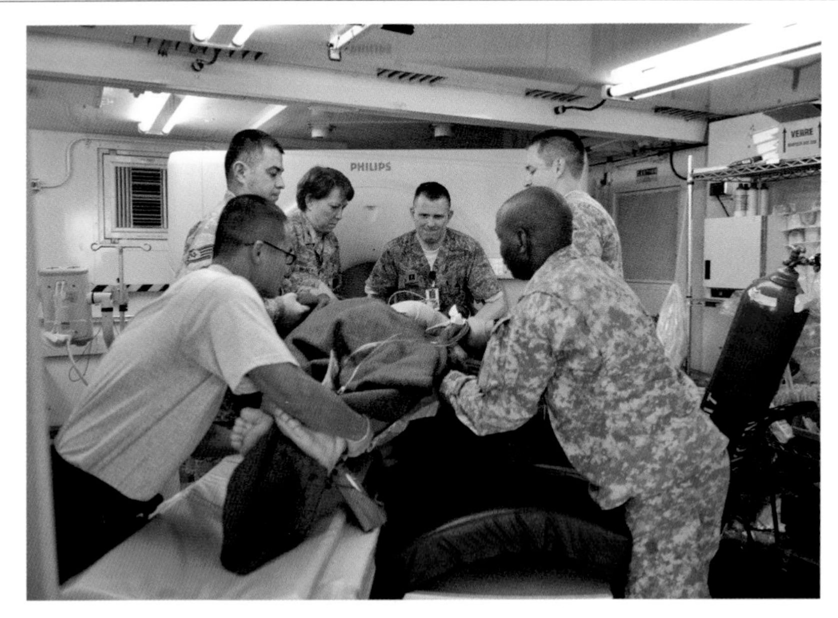

U.S. Army and Air Force medical personnel treating a wounded serviceman at the Bagram Air Base hospital. *DOD*

⁎ ⁎ ⁎

The phone rang at about eight o'clock in the morning. The sun was up and Jesseca was already starting to stir but not quite awake. She was scheduled to work the two-to-ten shift at the gym, so there was little need to jump out of bed and begin the day. As she rolled over and looked with half-opened eyes at the caller ID, she didn't recognize the strange array of numbers and assumed it was Brian calling from Afghanistan. She smiled reaching for the phone as she thought about the man she loved unconditionally.

"Hello."

"Yes, is this Jesseca Meyer, the wife of Staff Sergeant Brian Meyer?" asked the caller from Quantico, Virginia.

"Yes, this is she."

"Ma'am, I have some serious information to pass on to you."

"Okay," said Jesseca tentatively, her heart beginning to pound.

"Ma'am, are you sitting down?"

"What's going on?" said Jesseca, now with subdued panic in her voice.

"Your husband, Staff Sergeant Meyer, has been wounded in action and has received some serious injuries." The caller paused, then asked, "Are you ready to hear his injuries? Ma'am, I suggest you get a pen and paper to write this down."

"Okay!" Tears began to flood her eyes as her hand shook, preparing to write.

The caller continued: "While conducting a dismounted patrol northwest of Sangin, Helmand Province, Afghanistan, Staff Sergeant Meyer was struck by an improvised explosive device blast. Staff Sergeant Meyer was diagnosed by an on-scene corpsman with an amputation of the right leg above the knee, amputation of the right hand, and amputation of two fingers on his left hand. Staff Sergeant Meyer was medevac'd to Bastion Role III Medical Facility for higher-level treatment. Staff Sergeant Meyer was identified by his dog tags."

Jesseca's heart ached with a hurt so deep she thought it might never heal. Her mind was racing in so many directions she had trouble focusing on the call. She sat in stunned silence.

"Ma'am, are you still there?"

"Yes. Are you sure?" asked Jesseca, hoping against hope there had been a mistake.

"Yes, ma'am. Please know that we are available twenty-four/seven and you can call us for updates. He is in stable condition but will be transported to another hospital in Afghanistan."

She remembers getting out of bed, the phone still in her hand, sobbing as she walked out of the bedroom. The agony that seared her soul now numbed her body. She saw housemate Parker Blanche, an EOD colleague, standing in the hallway, staring at her.

"Is it Brian?" he asked, knowing the call wasn't good news.

Jesseca returned to her room, grasping at the reality confronting her; her mind taking her to dark places. She tried to call Heidi, multiple times, but it always went to voice mail. She then called Staff Sergeant Mark Zambon, one of Brian's EOD colleagues, a patient at Balboa who was struggling with his own losses.

In May 2010, while on his fifth combat deployment an IED initiator exploded in his left hand, traumatically amputating several joints on his fingers. Mark was medically evacuated and eventually treated at the Naval Medical Center San Diego, commonly referred to as Balboa.

But he wouldn't allow a few missing digits to end his career. Mark rehabilitated quickly and within five weeks was back to full duty, volunteering for a sixth deployment. He and Brian were part of the October mission.

In January 2011, while en route to a device discovered by Marines patrolling in Sangin, several Marines stepped through a pile of debris that had been swept by a combat engineer. Somehow the secreted device had remained undetected. Mark stepped on a pressure-plate IED and both legs were traumatically amputated above the knees. Twice in less than a year, he was a patient at Balboa.

Mark was in physical therapy when his phone rang and the call went to voice mail. When he spotted the missed call he checked his messages. The tears in Jesseca's voice were evident and he called her immediately. He understood what Brian was experiencing and helped Jesseca survive the shock of the early morning phone call. He explained the medical route Brian would be taking . . . Bagram to Landstuhl to Bethesda . . . the same journey he took twice. Although he offered words of encouragement, the unknown overwhelmed her.

Jesseca didn't know the full extent of Brian's wounds but she knew her husband was joining Mark and thousands like him who were the casualties of war, seldom covered in the media . . . those with crippling injuries requiring months, if not years, to recover the skills we too often take for granted like walking, talking, hearing, and thinking.

Later in the week, Mark and his roommate, Staff Sergeant Dave Lyon, another member of 1st EOD, who lost both of his legs in the spring of 2009 while serving in Afghanistan, took dinner to Jesseca. Between the two roommates, Mark and Dave had eleven combat deployments and no legs! While rightfully we hail those men who threw themselves on a grenade, saving the lives of others, we fail to appreciate those who risked everything to disarm that grenade. The work of Mark, Dave, Brian, and every other member of the EOD community saved thousands. As to his sacrifice, Dave Lyon seeks no sympathy: "I disarmed nearly four hundred IEDs during my numerous combat deployments; each device capable of killing or maiming. Wouldn't you give your legs to save the lives and limbs of your fellow Marines?"

Jesseca had learned in her relationship with Brian life is precious and each moment is to be savored. In the time they'd been together, she had attended countless memorial services for the many Marines killed in action. Of Brian's three roommates whom she met when she first traveled to San Diego that Halloween weekend, two were dead and the other, Bryan Carter, was a Purple Heart recipient who would later receive a Bronze Star for defusing by hand twenty-one IEDs in a single day. Her heart never hardened as her eyes scanned the room during those memorial services but she often wondered, "Who's next?" Then she could only pray, thanking God it wasn't "her Brian."

But now it was indeed "her Brian." Her EOD friends and civilian neighbor Aaron Root rallied. Amanda, Bryan Carter's fiancée, was already at the house but throughout the day the wives from 1st EOD came as well. Priscilla Maldonado and Cass Perez, wives whose husbands had been recently medically evacuated, arrived. They had received their calls earlier in the deployment. Christina Garibaldi, whose husband Jarret was Bryan Carter's partner, came by. Brandi Olson called. Her husband, Eric, also came home early from Afghanistan with combat-related wounds. With one month to go, Jesseca thought maybe they had dodged the proverbial bullet that had targeted so many of the EOD family. She was hoping the team would be winding down, minimizing the trips beyond the wire, but failed to grasp Brian would be disarming explosives until the day his replacement team arrived. The last week of the deployment was as dangerous as the first. She kept praying Brian would come home in one piece. But the nightmares continued and now with this call she learned not all of him was coming home.

The person who was one of the first to arrive that morning and the last to leave late into the night was Ann Schmalstieg. Ann never got a call; she received a notification team. She stayed by Jesseca's side until the early morning hours as they awaited a call from Brian that never came. Observing how Ann, a courageous Marine widow, handled grief gave Jesseca strength.

Jesseca managed to make it through the day, thanks to the support of friends, but she slept little that night. Finally, at four the next morning she was able to speak with Brian. The first thing her husband said was "I'm missing some body parts, babe."

* * *

At the U.S. Army's Landstuhl Regional Medical Center in Germany, Brian learned the medical diagnosis: a traumatic transfemoral amputation of the right leg, a traumatic transradial amputation of the right arm, the traumatic amputation of his left thumb and left index finger to later include the surgical amputation of his left middle finger, and the ruptured tympanic membranes in both ears. In short, he'd lost his right leg above the knee, his right arm below the elbow, all but two fingers on his left hand, had blown out both ear drums, and what was left of his arms and legs was riddled with shrapnel.

Jesseca envisioned the worst as the thoughts of his injuries flooded her mind. Sleep didn't come, maybe a couple of hours each night. What sleep she got came as the result of constant tears, exhausting a body demanding rest. It was hard to get out of bed. She lacked the motivation to do anything but worry. She longed to see him but at the same time was fearful of what she was about to see. He was a proud man and concerns grew as she questioned how he would see himself.

* * *

She now refers to it as "pi day." The mathematical designation for the ratio of the circumference of a circle to its diameter is 3.14. That day, March 14, or 3.14, changed their lives. Each night she would pinch herself, hoping and praying it was just a dream. But each time she awoke she knew the truth. Anger surfaced, sometimes at what were meant to be well-meaning gestures. People saying "it's going to be okay" had no idea—and neither did she—if things were really "going to be okay."

She kept updated on Brian's progress through her constant communication with the Marine Corps, who would be making travel plans for her to fly east and meet her husband in Bethesda, Maryland, at the National Naval Medical Center.

On Friday, after four long, anguish-filled days, Jesseca was to fly to Bethesda to meet Brian, who was arriving that day from Germany. Ann and Heidi came over to the house to help her pack but she was days ahead on the preparation, having packed early in the week. Ann gave her two handkerchiefs—"You're gonna need these." She then handed Jesseca an envelope containing a silver rosary and several prayers to guide her through the pain of the cross-country flight. Jesseca still refers to it as one of the best gifts she received along this torturous journey.

After boarding the plane it was as if the world collapsed and reality rose from the rubble. She attempted to hide the tears that continued throughout the flight, by throwing a hood over her head, so afraid someone would see her desperation, not wanting to share with anyone. She vowed on the flight to never let Brian see her cry in the hospital. She was hours from seeing her husband, not as she knew him when he left months earlier, but as he was now. What would she say? How would she react? And what would *he* say and how would *he* react? She feared in his desire to protect his new wife he might reject her, not wanting her to be burdened by the handicapped Brian. She was so afraid he might ask her to leave, never giving her a chance to express her love and devotion. Preparing for what she believed to be a real possibility, she pulled out her laptop and composed a letter expressing her intimate thoughts. In part, she wrote:

Jesseca was reunited with Brian at Walter Reed National Military Medical Center at Bethesda, Maryland. DOD

I wanted to start by letting you know that I love you with all my heart and soul. I will prove to you that I am a good and will always be a loyal wife. We will grow old together and this craziness will be nothing but a leaf blown by the wind. Please give me a chance to prove to you that I can make you happy. Please give us the chance to overcome this. We can and we will. I will be with you every step of the way. I will be patient and understanding. I know I might need a reminder sometimes so don't be afraid to remind me. Just like our beautiful yet ghetto wedding. . . .

"I offer you my solemn vow to be your faithful partner in sickness and in health, in good times and in bad, and in joy as well as in sorrow. I promise to love you unconditionally, to support you in your goals, to honor and respect you, to laugh with you and cry with you, and to cherish you for as long as we both shall live."

I promise you things will get better, but you must promise me you will never give up on life, because I will never give up on you. I fell in love with your personality, your gorgeous smile, your beautiful lips, and most importantly that absolutely amazing and most gorgeous heart of yours not the outside. Well, maybe your ass but we still have that!

I know that we will look at this one day, while we are laying down staring at the stars and realize how we can overcome anything that comes our way. We will have beautiful children, a beautiful home, and like I said before, we will rule the world! Like you always say baby . . . the world is our oyster.

It was after 1 A.M. when she walked into the intensive care unit at Bethesda. Through the window to his room she spied her husband, wrapped in blankets, his eyes closed, resting in bed, medical machines hooked to his body. Her stomach knotted and the tears came. She took a moment to compose herself, wiping away the tears, before entering the room. Taking a big breath, she entered with the words "My love, I've missed you so much!"

Brian opened his eyes and said, "I love you."

She remained at his side throughout the night, leaving the room only briefly to cry. Seeing him in the hospital brought back thoughts of the fun times she and Brian shared before the deployment. They led a fast-paced life, riding their motorcycles, rock climbing, four-wheeling, and taking long, romantic walks. She loved holding hands, whether on strolls at the beach or watching television. Looking at him in the bed at Bethesda, she knew life would be different. The

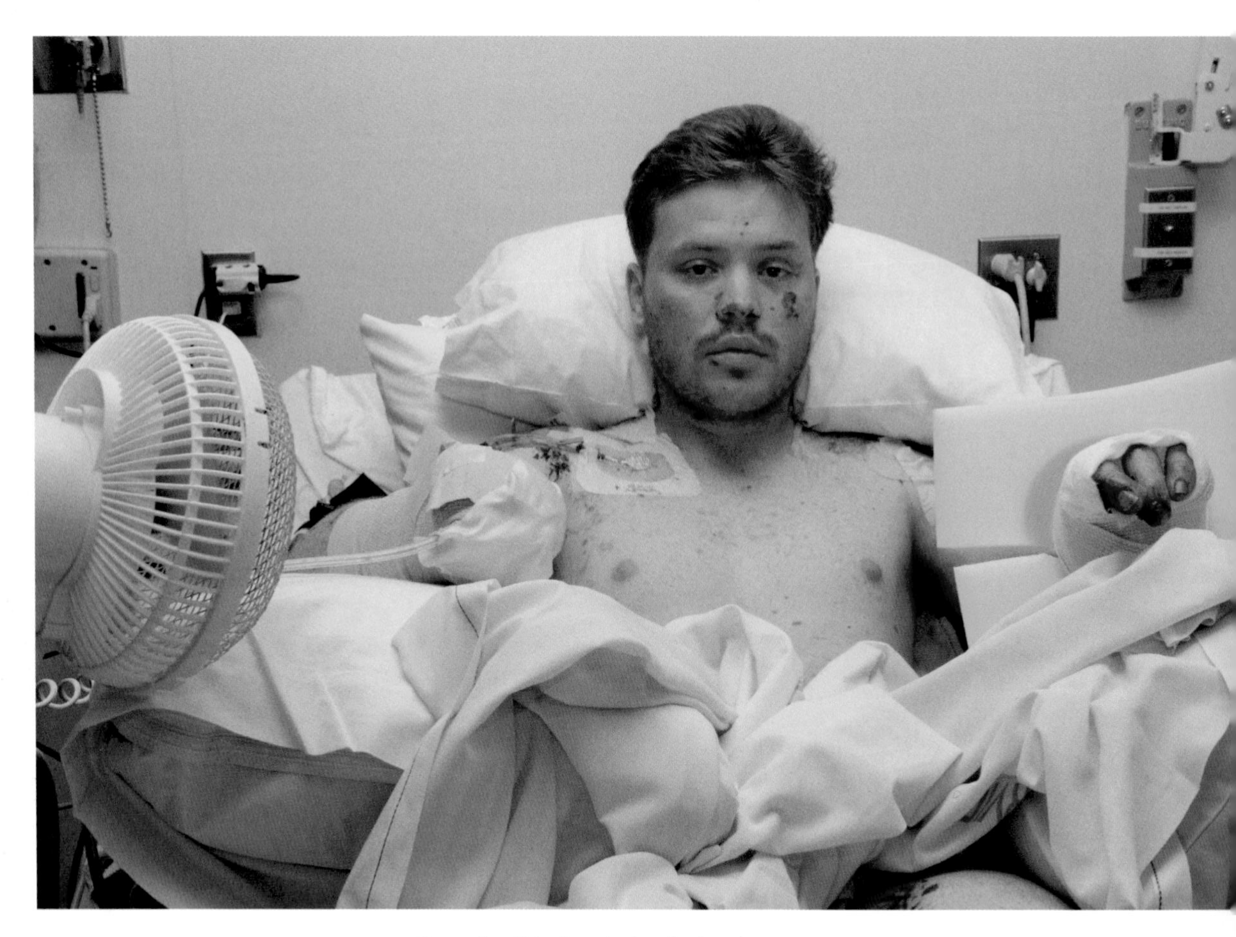

Days after Brian's arrival at Bethesda. *Jesseca Meyer*

Happy times before this last deployment. *Bryan Carter*

things she took for granted, like his gentle touch or his backrubs, were basically a thing of the past. But again with a million-dollar smile, she says she's grateful God left him with two fingers for her to hold.

Happy times before this last deployment. *Bryan Carter*

Jesseca spent virtually every moment in the room, lovingly performing those tasks often reserved for a nurse or aide. Whatever was called for she would do . . . empty a bedpan, give him a drink, grab a blanket, scratch his nose, clean him after he went to the bathroom. In a moment when they were alone in the room, lit only by the lights of the various machines monitoring Brian's condition, he said something that still brings tears to her eyes. "I don't expect you to stay with me. You didn't marry the Marine Corps and you certainly didn't marry this. If you want a divorce you can have it." She choked back the lump forming in her throat and read the letter she prepared on the plane. . . . It was the only time she cried in front of him at the hospital.

The days were long but nights longer. She was tired but rest seldom came. The mass-produced vinyl green chair in Brian's room provided little physical comfort. She would occasionally leave for a few hours, returning to the hotel room for a shower and to respond to texts,

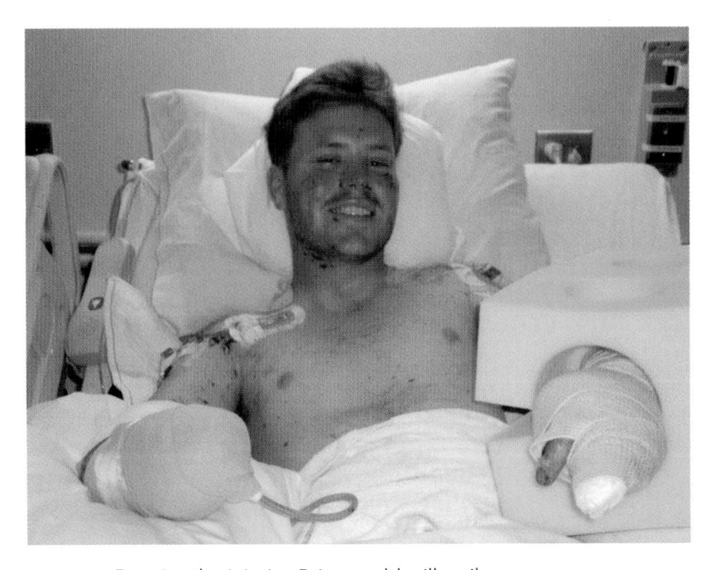

Despite the injuries Brian could still smile. *Jesseca Meyer*

Facebook messages, or phone calls. It was hard not to cry, pretending to be strong when in fact she ached, still questioning what the future held.

As Brian became stronger he was able to begin physical therapy. To watch him lift his arms and leg, such a simple act taken for granted, brought unbounded joy. But the surgeries were far from over.

In April 2011, while still a patient at Bethesda and after one of his dozens of surgeries, Brian awoke to a crowded hospital room packed with high-ranking Marine Corps officials, including General John F. Kelly, and civilian brass. Although Brian vaguely remembers the event, then–Secretary of Defense Robert Gates administered the oath as the combat-decorated Marine was promoted to gunnery sergeant. In describing his promotion, Brian later said with his patented smile, "It only cost me an arm and a leg."

Jesseca and Brian have found laughter to be a powerful medicine. Throughout the ordeal Jesseca

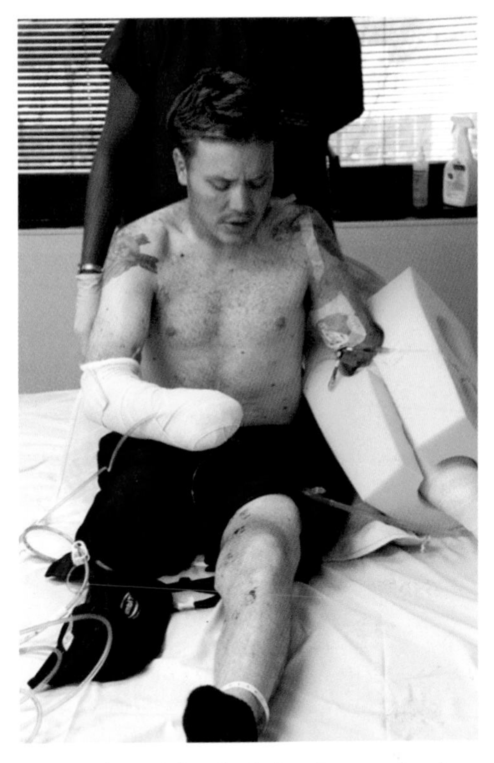

Brian begins the physical and occupational therapy, which is ongoing. *Jesseca Meyer*

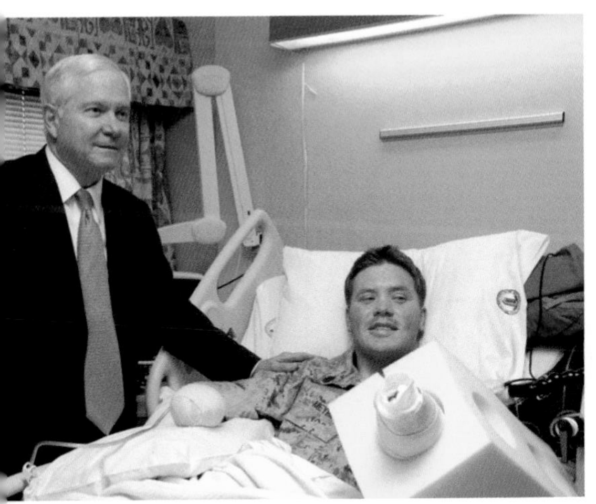

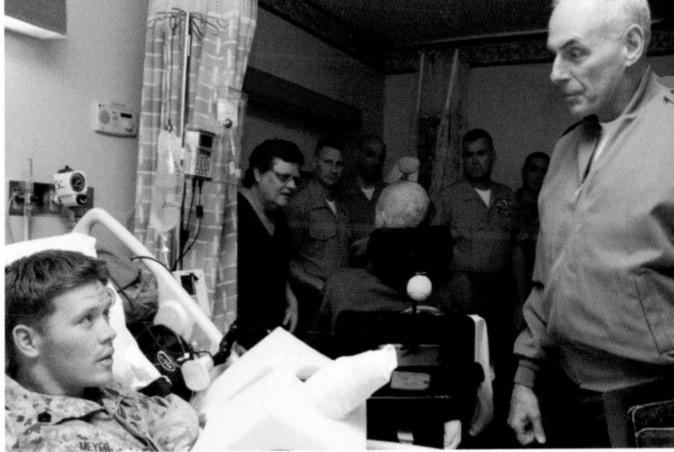

Left: Secretary of Defense Robert Gates on the day of Brian's promotion to gunnery sergeant. *Jesseca Meyer*
Right: General John F. Kelly at Brian's promotion. *Jesseca Meyer*

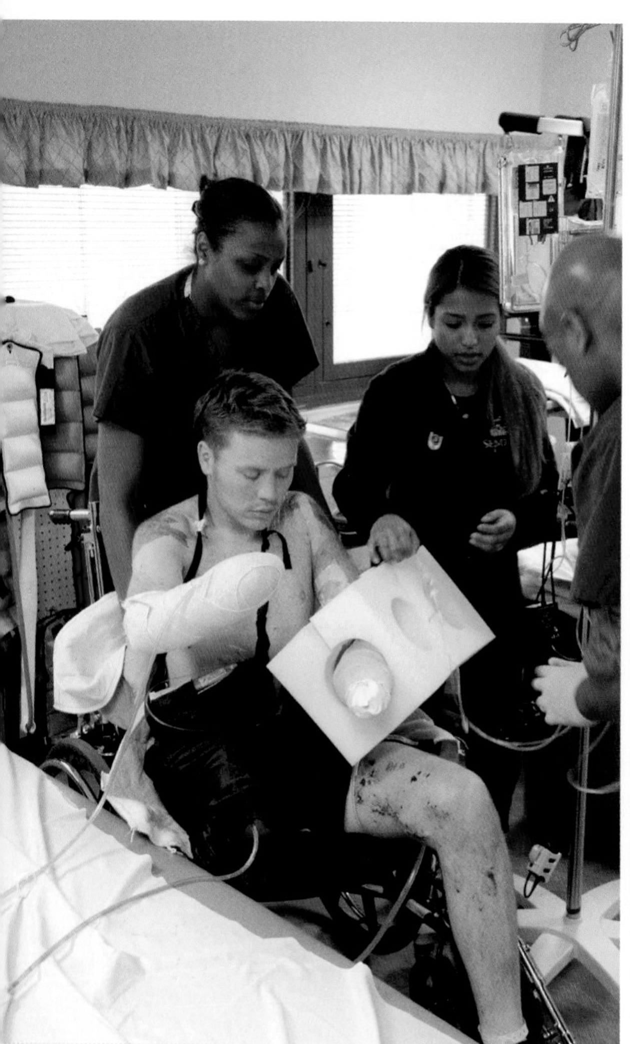

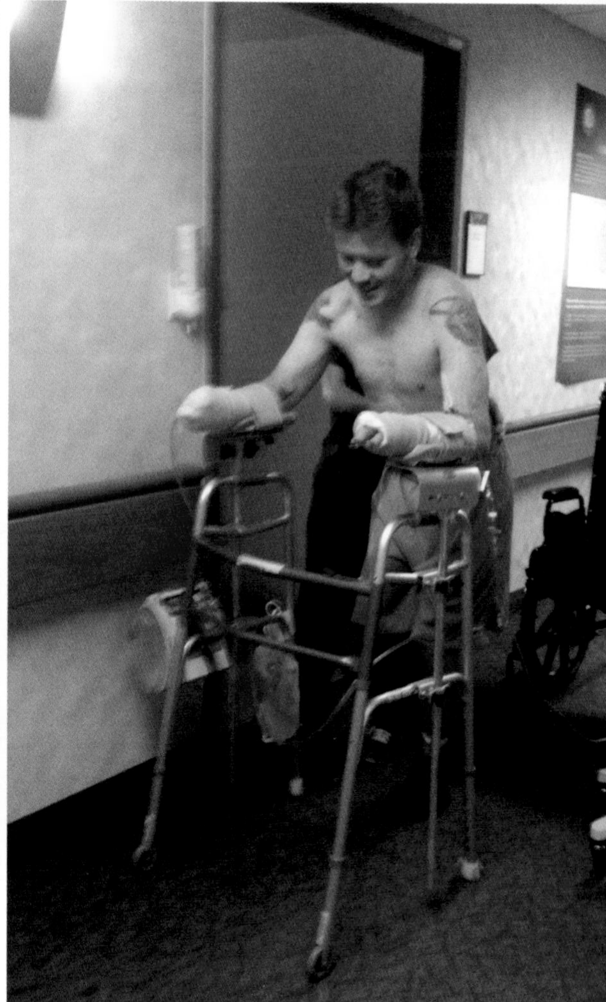

Brian begins the physical and occupational therapy, which is ongoing. *Jesseca Meyer*

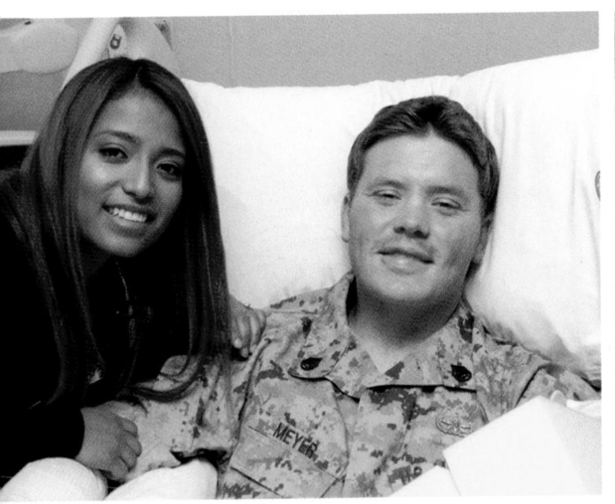

Left: A proud Jesseca on the day of Brian's promotion to gunnery sergeant. *Brian Meyer.* *Right:* The Purple Heart for EOD technician Gunnery Sergeant Brian Meyer. *Jesseca Meyer*

has learned to appreciate the value of friendship and surrounding herself with positive people. When she needed them most, friends and family stepped up and helped whenever they could, often just by providing a listening ear or a shoulder to cry on.

There is a new value to life when it's almost been taken from you. Jesseca and Brian have learned to appreciate the time they have together, never taking it for granted, enjoying every moment, trying not to sweat the minutiae. Theirs is a marriage built on a different kind of intimacy, not just the romance of the bedroom.

Jesseca entered the marriage with the idea it was a lifetime commitment, not just a renewable contract with an opt-out clause. She married Brian for better or for worse, and they have seen some "worse."

They have gone through more than most. Rather than bemoaning the experience, she views it as a privilege, forging a bond few marriages ever have the opportunity to encounter. She is still madly in love with the Brian Meyer she married on May 29, 2010. He may be missing a few limbs but his heart and mind remain the same.

His body continues to mend. Since March 14, 2010, Brian has been in the care of some of the Navy's most talented doctors and therapists, offering skilled treatment, encouragement, and love. Despite all he has encountered, he views a missing arm and leg as well as three missing fingers on his "good" hand as an "annoyance." "It takes me two minutes to do what used to take ten seconds but I'll adapt and I'll overcome." The love of his devoted wife will help him conquer the "annoyances" and the inevitable challenges facing this Wounded Warrior.

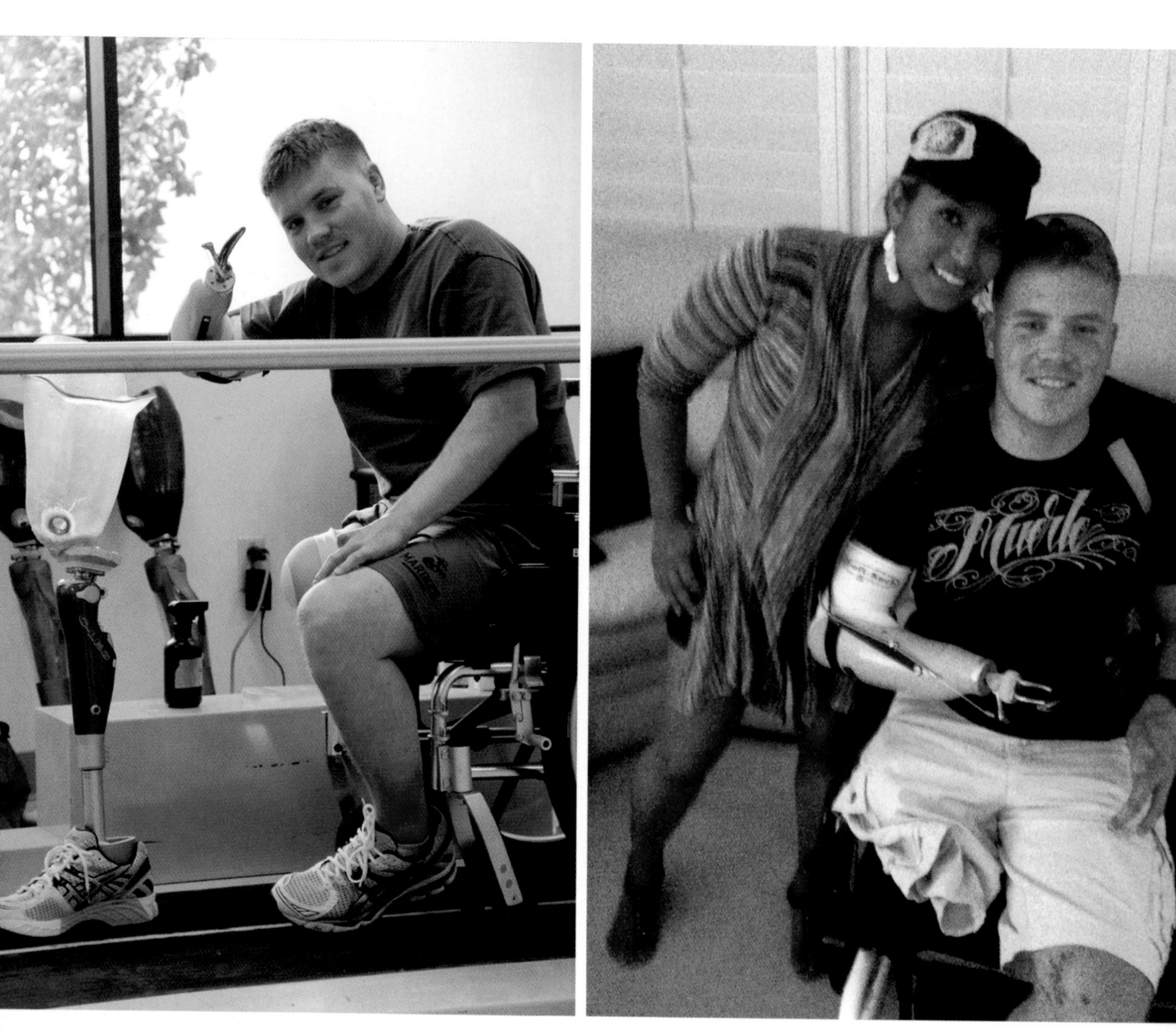

Left: Brian showing off his new hand and leg. *Jesseca Meyer*
Right: Brian and Jesseca still smiling through the "worse." *Bob Hamer*

At the races, Del Mar, California. *Bob Hamer*

Their first anniversary; a lot has changed in a year. *Brian Meyer*

Left: Brian and his 4x4 on the Outdoor Channel's *Off-Road Overhaul*. *Bob Hamer*. *Right:* Brian and Jesseca on the slopes, still active and still in love. *Brian Meyer*

☆

For every American serving overseas,

there are loved ones at home.

They too are America's heroes.

—OLIVER NORTH

☆

☆ ☆ ☆

A GOING-AWAY-FOOT PARTY

Taylor Linville

Charlie Linville's daughter, Taylor, was four and had a way of engaging everyone she met. Never shy, she was always ready to contribute to the conversation. She and her mom, Mandi, were standing outside Party City waiting for the doors to open. Several women were waiting as well. As many adults tend to do when a cute little girl is in their presence, one of the ladies directed a question to Taylor: "So what are you celebrating?"

Saying good-bye before the last deployment. *Mandi Linville*

Without hesitation Taylor responded, "My dad's having his foot cut off and we're having a going-away-foot party."

You could have heard a pin drop as jaws fell. The ladies looked to Mandi, who nodded. Some uncomfortable stammering followed before the lady inquired further and Taylor continued the conversation: "He got blown up by a terrorist in Afghanistan and he's having his foot amputated."

Charlie Linville and his wife, Mandi. *Mandi Linville*

Charlie and Mandi's daughter, Taylor. *Mandi Linville*

Taken immediately after the explosion. *Brian Meyer*

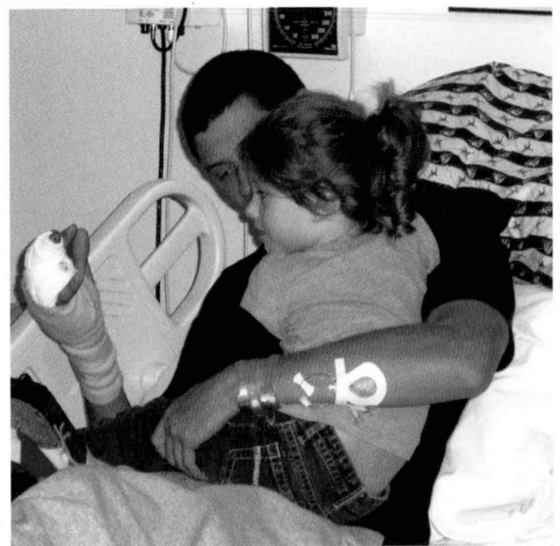

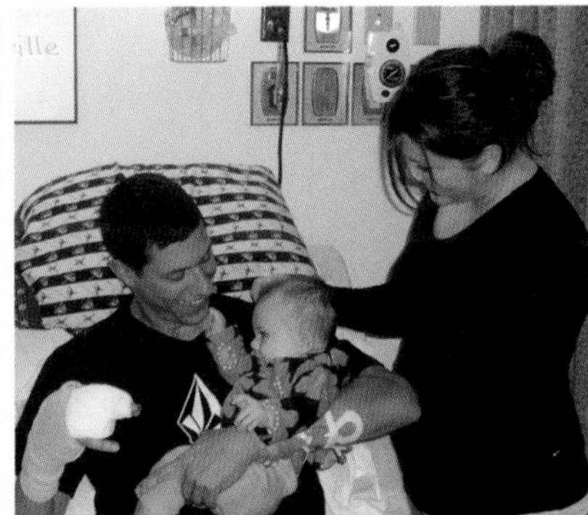

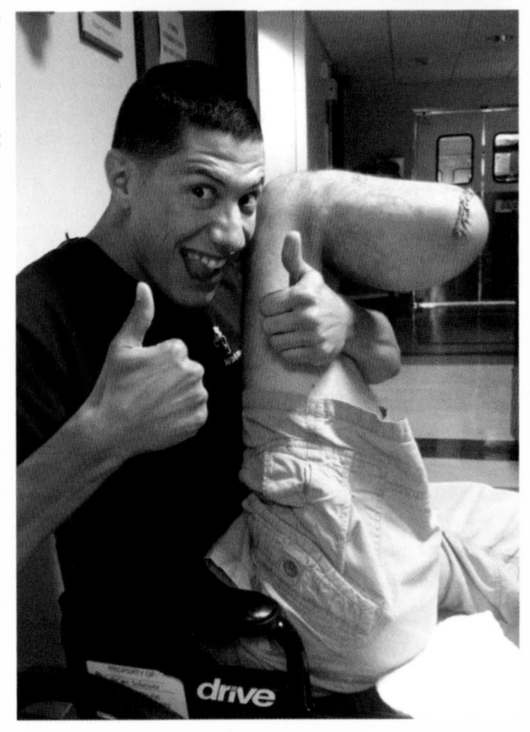

Top left: Taylor hugs her dad after being reunited following his return from Afghanistan. *Mandi Linville. Top right:* A proud father greets his youngest daughter. *Mandi Linville. Right:* The foot is gone but Charlie can still laugh. *Mandi Linville*

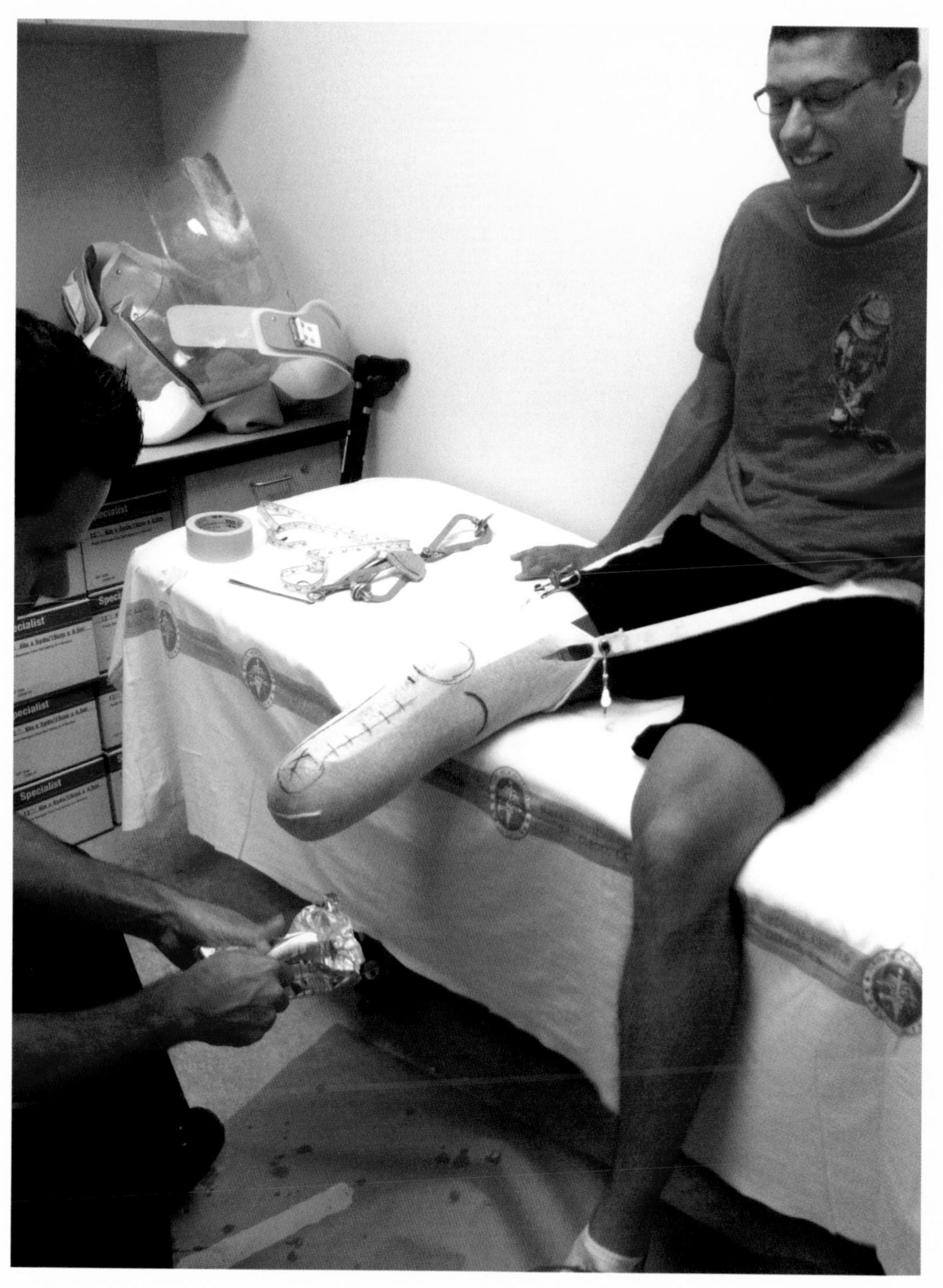

Being fitted for his prosthetic leg. *Mandi Linville*

The Linvilles with Oliver North at the Freedom Alliance 2012 Heroes Gala. *Freedom Alliance*

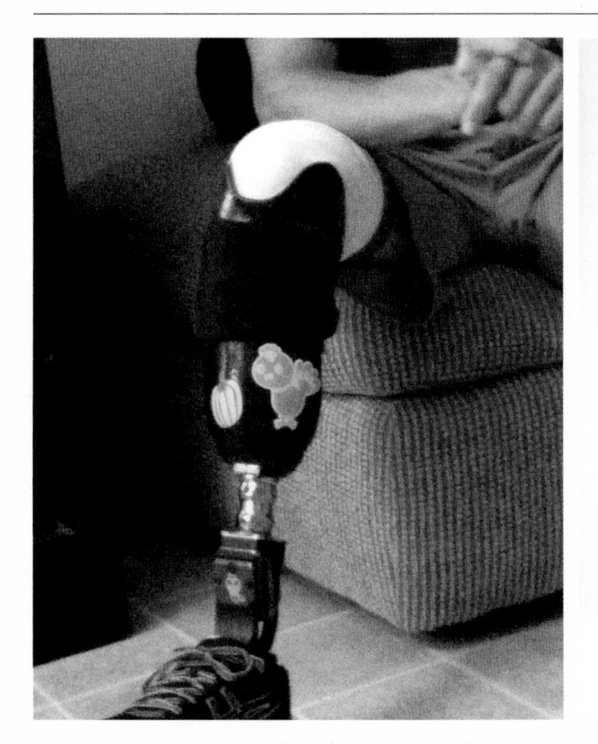

Left: Taylor and Dyllan helped decorate Daddy's new leg. *Mandi Linville*
Right: Charlie and his daughter Dyllan still smiling. *Challenged Athletes Foundation*

Tears began to form in the eyes of the ladies, now glued to this little girl who was so matter-of-fact about the tragedy. Finally the lady asked, "And how do you feel about that?"

"It's okay. He's going to be able to play with me again."

Mandi was living in Okinawa, Japan, with their two children when she received the call informing her of her husband's injuries. She relocated the family to San Diego as Charlie suffered through a half-dozen unsuccessful operations to salvage the right leg. Seventeen months later the limb was amputated. The trauma of her father having his leg amputated was lessened for Taylor, who had been around too many Marines with missing arms and legs, but she and her little sister, Dyllan, know firsthand the price of freedom.

Staff Sergeant Nick Sprovtsoff, his wife, Tasha, and their daughter, Lanie. *Tasha Sprovtsoff*

2

☆ ☆ ☆

IT WAS LONG ENOUGH TO LAST FOREVER

Nick and Tasha Sprovtsoff

As Tasha inched her way closer to the computer keyboard she peered out the living room window. Her soft brown eyes and huge smile welcomed the morning. It was almost eight, the sun was up, and there was just a hint of Southern California autumn in the air. At thirty-six weeks pregnant, a yoga exercise ball, rather than a chair, offered a modicum of relief for the lower back and hip pain she was experiencing. This morning she would sacrifice comfort to share her excitement. She logged on . . . September 29 . . . hoping her husband, Staff Sergeant Nick Sprovtsoff, was also logged on and they could Facebook chat. He was in his sixth month of a seven-month combat deployment and she was counting the days until his return.

On Wednesday she attended a wives briefing and it looked like Nick would be returning before "Tank" was born. Wanting to be surprised, Tasha wouldn't ask the doctor the sex of their second child. Before Lanie, their

A hero's resting place at Arlington National Cemetery. *Tasha Sprovtsoff*

precious fourteen-month-old daughter, was born Nick called her Tank, convinced they were having a boy. He dropped the nickname once he learned she was a girl but for a reason known only to Nick, he nicknamed her "Tuna." For now Tank would remain Tank unless he turned out to be a girl, then Nick could come up with a new nickname.

Tasha learned at the briefing Nick's replacement team was leaving that week, so it was only a matter of days before he'd be breaking down camp preparing to return home. Her original due date was October 23 but now the doctor was revising it to November 2. Nick would be with her for Tank's arrival!

When she determined Nick wasn't logged on she sent out a few emails telling friends Nick was coming home within weeks.

Tasha was eager to show her husband the house she had rented a few months earlier, just outside Camp Pendleton's back gate. It was in a nice neighborhood and offered a lot more room than the house they first rented when they moved to Oceanside a year and a half earlier. Besides, it was mold-free, a condition the previous landlord had no interest in correcting. The new landlord was a lot nicer, and the house was feeling like home even though a few boxes still needed to be unpacked.

The doorbell rang. It seemed too early for UPS, but she got up from the computer and made her way toward the front door, dodging the toys she failed to pick up the night before. While she was usually a meticulous housewife, pregnancy and playing the role of a single parent to an active toddler were taking their toll.

Dressed in a maternity top, a worn-out pair of Nick's Marine Corps sweat pants, and his Moosehead hoodie, she wasn't quite ready to receive company.

Tasha peered through the security peephole and saw six men in uniform: two Marines, a Navy chaplain, and three Navy corpsmen. She recognized John, a MARSOC (Marine Corps Forces Special Operations Command) EOD technician who served with Nick. Because she was still celebrating the news Nick might make it home before the baby was born, for a fleeting moment she thought the men were deliver-

Nick and Tasha. *Tasha Sprovtsoff*

ing good news. Then reality gripped her as her heart began to ache and her stomach knotted. This wasn't good news; this was a notification team!

As if somehow she could escape the news she was about to receive, she hesitated in opening the door. Her hand trembled as she reached for the doorknob, hoping beyond hope the men would be gone when she opened the door . . . they weren't.

"How are you doing today, ma'am?"

"I don't think I'm doing very well. I don't want to see you," she said, trying to maintain her composure but knowing her emotions were about to erupt.

"I know you don't, ma'am."

Tasha began to shake and John grabbed her elbow as the Marine escorted her to the couch, tears now flooding her face. "This can't be right; we're going to have a baby and we don't even know if it's a boy or girl."

The men offered comfort but she can't recall their exact words since the shock of the news blocked out much of what was said. Nick had been killed a day earlier but for a reason she still doesn't understand the men arrived first thing in the morning rather than the previous night.

A million thoughts consumed her. She knew the risks. She and Nick talked about it before each deployment but somehow she never believed she would get "the visit." Nick was too good at his job. He was a highly respected and highly decorated Marine. It was his experience and expertise that comforted her daily. She never dwelled on death because Nick shared so little of what he was doing, always bringing a sense of calm in their conversations. But in the back of her mind darkness lingered; she knew too many in this war who had sacrificed their lives and limbs.

After collecting herself as much as she could, which she admits wasn't much, Tasha asked, "What now?"

John questioned if there was anyone she would like to call to be with her.

She called friends Brittany and Amy but both calls went to voice mail. She wanted to call her mom but knew the Marines wanted someone to come over immediately. She thought about her friend Dana, but her husband, Thomas, had returned home that morning from his deployment and Tasha couldn't ruin their special day.

She searched her mind trying to come up with another name but her mind was awash with thoughts of Nick and Lanie and the baby growing inside her. She needed to process what was being asked of her, focusing on the immediate. She couldn't grieve as others might; she needed to protect Tank. "Stay calm, remember the baby," she thought as she tried to come up with the name of another friend who could help. The Marines weren't pushing, willing to stay as long as it took, but she wanted a friend right now . . . she needed a friend!

Then the phone rang. It was Brittany, the wife of Purple Heart recipient Jeff Rodriguez. Nick and Jeff went to EOD school together and were now stationed at Camp Pendleton. The couples were best friends and Brittany loved Lanie, always welcoming the opportunity to hold her. Brittany was out the door before ending the call.

Now a Gold Star wife, a distinction no one seeks, Tasha called her mom and in between tears said, "Nick was killed yesterday."

"What?" asked her mom.

Tasha repeated the news.

"We're on our way" was all her mother said and the conversation ended. Tasha had heard what she needed to hear. By seven o'clock that night, Tasha's family rallied from Washington State, Colorado, and Nevada.

Her Marine Corps family rallied as well. Jesseca Meyer, whose husband, Brian, came home early from his deployment having left an arm, a leg, and several fingers in Afghanistan, arrived by midafternoon and fixed dinner as family and friends crowded into the home.

* * *

When you think of a combat-tested Marine who was awarded a Bronze Star with valor, the Purple Heart, a Navy–Marine Corps Achievement Medal with valor, the Army Commendation and Army Achievement medals, and two Combat Action Ribbons, you think high school football star, all-state wrestler, or rugby player. Seldom does a high school tennis player and varsity bowler come to mind, but don't be fooled by the freckles and mischievous ear-to-ear grin. Nick Sprovtsoff was a true warrior. The medals were awarded by the military but the highest accolades came from the Marines he knew and with whom he served, who described him as a "consummate professional," a "man's man," and a "Marine's Marine."

Bill Tenny, Nick's best friend while growing up in Davison, Michigan, a Flint suburb, called Nick "smart, competitive, and somewhat of an adrenaline junkie." He enjoyed snowboarding, dirt biking, and competitive paintball. Nick was a high school entrepreneur with his own lawn care service and snow removal business. Never afraid of hard work, he spent summers working for a construction company and always welcomed a challenge. Driven to be the best, he wanted to win, never wasting time complaining about how difficult a task was. Even in high school he was mission-focused. When he thought about his immediate future, he wanted to be a Marine and it seemed like a perfect fit.

* * *

Tasha, the oldest of four children, was born in Colville, Washington, a small town sixty-five miles north of Spokane, near the Canadian border. Her family's financial success wasn't immediate. She lived with her parents and three siblings in a double-wide mobile home until she was nine, when the family moved to a much larger house, reflecting her parents' hard work and subsequent success. A straight-A student in high school, Tasha was captain of the school's dance team. She then earned a degree in graphic design from the Art Institute of Seattle.

Engaged to her high school sweetheart, she broke off the relationship shortly before the wedding. Wanting to get on with life and away from some bad memories, she took her sister's advice. Elizabeth was going to college in Montana and Tasha moved in, finding work in retail sales. When Tasha expressed her frustration one evening on the phone when a promised job in management hadn't materialized, her mom mentioned a graphic design position with the Yellow Pages in Hawaii. The thought of moving to Oahu and working in her chosen field intrigued the twenty-three-year-old, who soon relocated.

The new job was demanding, with long hours and plenty of work. Tasha had been on the island about a year and a half and dated some, but no one had held her interest for long. Her sister Alaina also moved to Hawaii and the two spent what little free time Tasha had exploring Honolulu's nightlife.

One evening she and her sister were at Nashville Waikiki, one of their favorite hangouts, a country-western bar in the heart of Waikiki. Tasha noticed a ruggedly handsome guy on the other side of the bar. There was a just a hint of auburn hair in his military-style cut, and at six feet two, 210 pounds, he carried himself as confident but not cocky. Throughout the evening she caught him glancing her way. Tasha kept waiting for him to make the first move but he never did, even though the furtive glances continued. She was standing

Nick and Tasha celebrate at the annual Marine Corps Birthday Ball. *Tasha Sprovtsoff*

close to the restrooms and when Nick suddenly exited the men's room, she grabbed his arm and introduced herself. The stalemate was broken and by the end of the evening he invited her to the Marine Corps Birthday Ball the next weekend.

Nick, a crew chief on an amphibious assault vehicle, later admitted he went to the bar hoping to find a date for the ball and ended up with a wife.

Tasha was putting in twelve-, fourteen-, even twenty-hour days with her graphic design job and was at the point of exhaustion. Shortly after agreeing to go to the ball, she told her mom's best friend she was thinking of canceling the date but Evelyn encouraged her to go. "This could be the guy you're going to marry," she told Tasha.

Her first Marine Corps Birthday Ball was an occasion to remember; the Marines in their dress blues, women dressed to the nines, ceremony, tradition, and lots of alcohol. Even though it was their first date, Nick kept introducing her as his girlfriend and she liked the title. Within two weeks of dating she knew there was something different about this one; he was a gentleman who treated her like a lady and she was in love.

Nick had two previous combat deployments to Iraq and they both knew a third one was in the future. By now she was telling her parents about the macho Marine she'd been dating for several months. When they came to Hawaii to celebrate Tasha's birthday, they met their future son-in-law for the first time. Though he was bruised and battered from the Marine Corps martial arts program, they welcomed him with open arms.

He was in love as well. There was the obvious physical attraction but Nick was impressed by a work ethic they both shared. Life as a Marine Corps wife isn't easy, the "toughest job in the Marines," if you believe the bumper stickers. He needed to prepare Tasha for the hardships they could be facing. Ours was a nation at war and there was the constant training in preparation for the next deployment; long periods of separation were a certainty. They both knew the moments they would have together needed to be valued. Every word needed to be said and every kiss needed to be given because the times together would be far too brief. She said it then as she says it now: "I'd rather have five minutes with you than a lifetime with anyone else."

Although Tasha was ready to spend the rest of her life with Nick, he wanted to make sure the relationship could withstand a deployment. They had been dating about a year when he left for Afghanistan.

Called an Embedded Training Team, or ETT, the Marines served as mentors molding Afghan soldiers into disciplined military units capable of conducting counterinsurgency operations. In forming the teams, the Marines drew experienced officers and noncommissioned

Top: Nick at a military outpost in the Hindu Kush. *Tasha Sprovtsoff*
Bottom: Nick during his final deployment in Helmand Province. *Tasha Sprovtsoff*

officers from a variety of military occupational specialties. Nick had proven himself in previous deployments and was selected for a team.

By now Tasha was growing tired of the long hours required in her job and decided to return to Colville while Nick was gone. She joined her dad in the family business and learned firsthand the pain of separation. Although she emailed Nick every night, he was able to respond only on an infrequent basis, Internet access not being readily available. The phone calls were minimal. She missed his voice but cherished the occasional email she received, knowing with each communication how much she wanted to share her life with him.

He didn't talk much about the dangers and it was only after he returned from the deployment she learned of his Bronze Star for bravery.

The team was mentoring a company of Afghan National Army (ANA) soldiers tasked with disrupting terrorist forces operating in the Watapor Valley. On July 5, 2007, the unit air-assaulted into Tsanger Village. Shortly after Nick set up his ANA platoon, he learned of a pending attack. Within minutes as many as eighty enemy fighters assaulted, with Nick's position receiving the brunt of the onslaught. Without regard for his own safety he rushed to assist an ANA RPG gunner who was seeking cover. Nick grabbed the RPG and extra rounds and maneuvered himself into position as he was receiving sniper, machine-gun, and RPG fire. Nick halted the enemy attack with well-aimed RPG fire, allowing his medics to aid three severely wounded ANA soldiers, ultimately saving their lives. Nick then returned to his previous position and rallied the remaining ANA troops, maneuvering his men to flank the enemy, breaking the attack and inflicting severe casualties on the assaulting enemy force. His actions allowed the medics to treat the additional wounded ANA soldiers. This fighting went on for more than two and a half hours as Nick continued to engage the enemy while under intense small arms fire, maneuvering his men through dangerous terrain, enabling the wounded to receive treatment and disrupting the enemy assault. The Bronze Star citation concludes in part, "Sgt. Sprovtsoff's actions showed extreme courage and gallantry . . . and total disregard for his own safety during the 48-hour fight. His valorous actions . . . showcase his personal courage, dedication to duty, and commitment to his fellow Service Members."

When Nick returned from the deployment his first stop was Colville. He had been facing down terrorists on a daily basis for months, but Tasha's mom noticed he was fidgeting nervously and wondered if it was fear. Her dad, who was leaving on a hunting trip, had just locked his guns in the truck when Nick cautiously approached him in the driveway. Nick then asked for Tasha's hand in marriage. Receiving the answer he hoped to hear, her dad said yes with no shots ever being fired!

Nick proposing to Tasha at the Marine Corps Birthday Ball. *Tasha Sprovtsoff*

Tasha and Nick returned to Hawaii. Nick's unit was celebrating the Marine Corps birthday at the Hilton Hawaiian Village. On Friday evening, as they headed to the cocktail hour, Nick suddenly remembered he'd forgotten his "credit card" and needed to return to the room. In fact, he had forgotten something else.

When he returned, he padded toward Tasha and tapped her on the shoulder. As she turned he got down on one knee.

"Hey, baby, will you marry me?"

With a tear of hope forming in her eye, she said, "Are you serious?"

"You see the ring, don't you?"

That night Tasha enjoyed semi-celebrity status as women in the ladies' room asked, "Are you the girl who just got engaged?" She answered by proudly displaying her new diamond.

On Monday, before they could even begin to discuss wedding plans, Nick shared some troubling news. The team that replaced his ETT had lost a man. Marine Sergeant Phillip Bocks was killed in an ambush following a meeting with tribal elders in the eastern Afghanistan mountains. The team was one man short and a replacement had to be found. As Nick explained, the choices were few. Two members of the previous team had the skills needed to replace Sergeant Bocks: Nick and a married Marine with children. Nick told Tasha he was the only viable selection. She didn't want him to leave but it was hard to argue with his commitment to duty.

With orders back to Afghanistan imminent, they decided a civil ceremony at the courthouse in Hawaii made the most sense. On November 19, 2007, ten days after the proposal, Tasha and Nick were married by a judge in front of a witness whose name they never learned. Two days later Nick left for Afghanistan.

Following this fourth combat deployment Nick was slated for recruiting duty, a safer assignment but one he didn't want. Convincing reluctant mothers their sons should join the military wasn't in his nature. He found an alternative but the price was steep . . . he became an Explosive Ordnance Disposal technician, a real-life Hollywood "Hurt Locker."

En route to the EOD school in Florida, the two returned to Colville and celebrated with the big wedding Tasha had dreamed of having.

A year later on the day Nick graduated, earning the coveted joint service badge designating an EOD tech, known as the "EOD Crab," Tasha learned she was pregnant with Lanie. The world

Nick and Tasha at their wedding in Colville, Washington. *Kebbie Hess Green*

The coveted EOD "Crab." *USMC Sgt. Peter Pearson*

seemed right as they headed to Camp Pendleton, Nick with orders to MARSOC and Tasha carrying their first child. Though the Marine Corps has a rich tradition of performing extraordinary combat missions and prides itself on being "first to fight," it is new to the special ops arena. MARSOC was officially activated in February 2006. Fighting alongside Navy SEALs and the Army's Delta Force, Green Berets, and Rangers, the Marine Corps joined the shadow-warrior community.

The training was intense and Nick spent few nights at home. With the passion and professionalism he showed throughout his career, he wanted to be the best. At the Basic Reconnaissance Course, Nick won the Iron Man award, another indication of his excellence. When he wasn't in the field at Camp Pendleton he was attending schools throughout the nation, acquiring the skills needed both as a special ops Marine and an EOD technician. Sometimes he was able to share where he was going but oftentimes he couldn't. For those trips he would tell Tasha, "I'm going to Kansas," and she would smile at their secret code.

Nick was, however, in town for Lanie's birth, sitting at Tasha's side for twenty hours of labor and the subsequent complications. The first three weeks he was there for every bath and most

Lanie and her dad on his motorcycle. *Tasha Sprovtsoff*

dirty diapers. For a guy trained in the art of war he was a gentle giant when it came to handling the newest Sprovtsoff. But the time went quickly and he was forced to return to training, preparing with his men for the next deployment. He looked forward to the weekends he could be home, playing the new dad and watching Lanie grow. He knew his fifth deployment would be coming soon and he cherished the time—too little—he had with his growing family.

* * *

Life is approached differently for the family of a combat veteran due to return to the battlefield. The Sprovtsoffs knew too many military friends killed and maimed and didn't want to wait until Nick returned to begin thinking of a second child. Even though Lanie was only a few months old, they wanted another child.

For Tasha's birthday the family went to Palm Springs, California, to be with her parents, who spend part of every winter there. Tasha suspected she was pregnant but laughingly said that while she had been pregnant on her twenty-ninth birthday, she refused to know if she was on her thirtieth! Up early to take the test the day *after* her birthday, it came back positive. When a second test also proved positive she texted Nick, who was now golfing with her dad, "Yep, I'm pregnant." Nick kept the secret from her dad, letting Tasha share the good news, but admitted his drives weren't nearly as straight nor his putting as accurate after receiving the message.

That night the room exploded with excitement after they pulled her dad aside, asking, "Next year, can we bring two babies to Palm Springs?"

Tasha admits the first time she learned she was pregnant she was scared, but Nick was thrilled. The second time they were both thrilled . . . although dark thoughts lingered in the back of her mind.

Now with MARSOC, Nick looked far from the regulation Marine she had met a few years earlier. His hair was longer and he wore a scruffy beard.

When Nick deployed in March 2011, Tasha remained in Oceanside with her military friends, many from the EOD community. She kept busy being a young mom and preparing for their sec-

Top and bottom: Nick in Afghanistan. *Tasha Sprovtsoff*

ond child. She was able to email Nick daily but recalls only about five phone calls and a handful of Skype sessions during the deployment.

She knew only that Nick was in Helmand Province, never the specific town or village. His emails were short as he often apologized for not having much to say; there was so much he couldn't tell her. He might mention it was a hard day but Tasha knew better than to ask. As Tasha describes it, "We had two rules: I was on a need-to-know basis, trusting him to decide what I needed to know, and I wouldn't ask questions I didn't want answers to." The emails centered on the children: what Lanie was doing, how she was changing, new-baby updates, and names for their second child. As with every deployment, Tasha emailed him every night and on most days she would get a response.

As the months passed without incident she continued to hope for his safe return. Even though she avoided most media outlets, she couldn't help but know the dangers facing her husband and his men. The Marine Corps is a tight-knit community, a family; injury and death plagued her friends and neighbors.

Nick's MARSOC team was part of a village stabilization program initiated in 2010. Operating under the authority of Afghanistan's Ministry of Interior, local leaders selected candidates for the Afghan Local Police (ALP) from those living in their towns and villages. Special operations units were deployed to mentor the ALP into becoming a first line of protection for the Afghan people, a "hometown civil defense force."

Until Nick's death, Tasha knew little about what he was doing. As she later learned, during this deployment Nick disarmed by hand nearly forty IEDs discovered by his MARSOC teammates or the ALP. The village was a hotbed of Taliban activity and almost daily the mud hut compound in which the team lived was attacked by gunfire, grenades, or mortars.

Although the team had been casualty-free, several ALP had been killed or injured. That was about to change.

On September 28, the ALP made a suspicious discovery: loose dirt with wires protruding from the ground. The team was called out and Nick prepared to do the job he was trained to do: disarm a lethal mechanism planted by terrorists. The team set up a perimeter around the site, a safe distance from the suspected device. Nick, working alone, cautiously moved forward, approaching the disturbed earth. He was able to separate out the component parts of the IED, attaching a rope to the main charge. After retreating a safe distance he pulled on the rope but the device failed to detonate. He cautiously waited before approaching the device a second time. As he returned to the device to reevaluate his find, he stepped on a second IED, one of seven discovered at the checkpoint. Hell rained down as the earth shook, with dust, dirt, and debris flying everywhere.

Top: Nick carrying an EOD "Pack-Bot" used to detect and disarm IEDs. *Tasha Sprovtsoff*
Left: Sweeping for buried IEDs. *Tasha Sprovtsoff*

Nick on guard outside an Afghan compound where marijuana flourishes. *Tasha Sprovtsoff*

With little regard for his own life, the team's Navy corpsman raced in to do his job, one of the most dangerous in the military, rescuing fallen Marines. Time was of the essence. Nick was catastrophically injured. Without prompt medical assistance and a rescue helicopter getting him to a hospital immediately, death seemed certain. The corpsman was able to render aid, applying tourniquets that stemmed much of the blood loss from the missing limbs, but Nick's life hung in the balance. As the corpsman was attempting to carry Nick's wounded body to safety, Staff Sergeant Christopher Diaz, a Marine dog handler, and Army combat medic James A. Butz rushed in to assist. A second device detonated, killing all three and seriously injuring the corpsman. The men were only twelve days from wrapping up a seven-month combat deployment; now their families were joining the growing community of those who have sacrificed loved ones in the name of freedom.

★ ★ ★

After the notification team left and friends and family arrived, Tasha needed to make some difficult decisions. She had flown to Washington State a week earlier to attend an NFL game honoring Army Staff Sergeant Wyatt Goldsmith, a high school friend killed a few months earlier in Afghanistan. It was uncomfortable to fly and she knew she was nearing the time when the doctors were going to prohibit her travel.

Tasha wanted to honor Nick's wishes of being buried at Arlington National Cemetery but she was thirty-six weeks pregnant and no one could give her the time frame in which all this might happen. It was devastating to think of not being there for the funeral but postponing the burial for months seemed unrealistic. Fortunately, the Marine Corps worked hard to accommodate Tasha's needs.

The day after Tasha was notified of Nick's death, she and her mom flew to Dover Air Force Base in Delaware to receive his body. As if the heavens were crying over the loss, Tasha stood in a cold rain for Nick's 3 A.M. arrival, welcoming him home from his final deployment. She returned to California later in the day, still uncertain as to when and where he would be buried, as the paperwork made its way through Washington's bureaucratic matrix.

On Monday, while in her bedroom, she received the call . . . Nick was going to be buried on Thursday at Arlington, the resting place he deserved. The family was standing in the kitchen when she walked out of the bedroom. "We got it," she said and burst into tears, relieved and proud.

On Wednesday eleven family members and friends flew from San Diego to Washing-

Nick Sprovtsoff given a hero's return at Dover Air Force Base at 3 A.M. *DOD*

ton, D.C., joining others who gathered from around the country. With such late notice, Tasha was pleased so many were able to make it. Luke Cournoyer, the corpsman on Nick's first Afghanistan deployment, accompanied her on a long walk, giving her a chance to talk with a trusted friend.

In addition to being buried at Arlington, Nick had voiced two other desires. He wanted his hometown friend Bill Tenny to receive his Springfield XD .45-caliber pistol and he wanted his motorcycle to go to Luke; testaments to a lifelong friendship and one forged in combat.

That night most of the guests went out for dinner and drinks. Tasha stayed in her room, partly to rest for what she knew was going to be a very long and difficult day, and because no one asked her to accompany them. Uninterrupted sleep was eluding her; too many trips to the bathroom. This night was no different, only every time she would lie down the same thoughts flooded her mind: "I can't believe this is happening . . . this can't be real . . . you don't have time to think about this right now . . . the baby needs you to sleep . . . breathe in and out . . . my back hurts . . . Nick would have rubbed it perfectly." She would fall asleep, only to awaken again to go to the bathroom and begin the process anew.

On Thursday morning, October 6, she was up early. It had been one week since she'd been notified of Nick's death and today was the funeral. Her world stood still yet raced beyond reality. The black dress she brought didn't fit properly, Tank taking up too much room. Trying to remain calm, her emotions almost spent, she found that the black pants she had also brought would work; one more stress eliminated.

Tasha still reflects on her uneasiness of shopping within a few days of her husband's death. Back in Oceanside, her mom and sisters had accompanied her to the mall. At the maternity store, when the clerk asked what she was shopping for she replied "black," thankful there was no further inquiry. Later at the mall she saw Jen, the wife of one of the Marines who had come to her door as part of the notification team. There was a long, heartfelt hug and accompanying tears, as Tasha felt the need to explain she had nothing to wear to Nick's funeral, fearful she'd be judged for going on a shopping spree while she should have been mourning.

When they arrived at the funeral home, the lobby was filled with Marines wearing their dress blue uniforms. Tasha couldn't make eye contact, afraid of losing control, but with quick glances she recognized many. Throughout the service she fought to keep her composure. Master Sergeant Kris Donald, Nick's mentor in EOD school who arranged for Nick to avoid recruiting duty, flew in from Okinawa and gave the eulogy. Tasha's family bought his ticket when military flights couldn't guarantee his arrival on time.

Nick laid to rest at Arlington National Cemetery. *Caryssa Hendricks*

Following the service, the pallbearers loaded the casket into the hearse, then proceeded through the District of Columbia to the cemetery. Arriving at Arlington, seeing the crowds, Tasha remembered this most hallowed ground was also a tourist attraction. As one of her sisters pointed out, Nick would be honored daily by Americans paying their respect.

After the flag-draped casket was loaded onto the horse-drawn caisson, everyone except Tasha walked to the grave site. She hated not being part of that walk and joining in the procession with Nick, but the pregnancy was taking its toll. She rode to the site in the limousine.

As she described it, the graveside service "was beautiful and moving and gut-wrenching." In a final tribute, the Sergeant Major of the Marine Corps presented her with the flag. As a last good-bye, Tasha laid her rose on Nick's casket. Even though she was heartbroken and devastated, a sense of pride accompanied every emotion; her military hero was at peace.

Once she returned to California she was overwhelmed by the outpouring of support she received. Friends, neighbors, even complete strangers showered her with gift cards and meals.

Both births were natural, without any medication. Unlike the twenty-hour labor for Lanie, Tank, who was almost two weeks late, arrived ten minutes after Tasha reported to the birth center; her mom was still putting coins in the parking meter. On November 9, one day before the Marine Corps' birthday, Nicholas Tank Sprovtsoff entered the world. He was all boy. At seven pounds, twelve ounces, and twenty-two inches long, his hint of auburn hair reminded many of his father.

☆ ☆ ☆

Whether it was as a husband, father, or Marine, Nick Sprovtsoff recognized the need for excellence, always striving to be the best.

He valued his role as warrior, believing in the mission, his men, and his country. He was part of a brotherhood united in the cause of freedom; watchmen standing on the wall.

As he prepared to leave for his last deployment someone told him to "stay safe and keep your head down." Although he knew they meant well, he smiled and nodded, but later told Tasha he hated it when people said that to him. If he were going over there just to stay safe and keep his head down he might as well stay home, because he wouldn't be doing his job; danger was an implied condition of every mission statement.

One afternoon shortly after Nick's death, Tasha was sitting in the backyard with her parents when the casualty assistance officer delivered the initial shipment of Nick's personal effects. It wasn't much; the bulk of the materials—his books, photos, letters, even the clothing he wore into battle—would come later. But for now she held his wedding ring and the contents of his wallet. She came across a folded piece of paper. In Florida, while Nick was attending EOD school, Tasha would awaken early every morning to fix his breakfast and pack his lunch. Occasionally she'd include a note expressing her love, knowing it probably embarrassed her Marine. As she unfolded the paper she recognized the writing. A smile formed as a tear began to track her cheek. Two years earlier she'd written "three reasons why I love you." Now she learned Nick carried that note with him wherever he went. She carefully refolded the note and placed it in her wallet, taking it wherever she goes, keeping their love alive.

For a long time she was able to put her grieving on hold, daily living keeping her occupied. Being a busy mother of two made it easier to cope with the loss. Even though Lanie and Tank are still too young to understand, Tasha fights hard to keep from breaking down in front of them. It isn't always easy, especially when Lanie asks when her daddy is coming home. When those moments come Tasha cradles the toddler in her arms and says, "Daddy is deployed to heaven. We can talk to him anytime we want and he can hear us. Someday we will see him again." More questions will come as the children get older, and she can only hope her answers assuage the hurt. Maybe because of the tears and anguish, she is stronger through the journey, but even when the pain and emotions spill over and she loses it in the quietness of her room, she feels Nick comforting her.

There are still the dreams of Nick, snuggling in bed, as they tell each other of their love. She can feel his arms providing that safety and security for which she longs . . . she feels his presence.

Losing Nick has been traumatic. The wound is deep and will not heal anytime soon. It has cut Tasha to her very core but she has fantastic memories. There is the joy, laughter, and love of

Lanie at her first Fourth of July celebration after Nick's death. *Dana Jones*

Tasha, Lanie, and Tank at the ocean. *Kristi Moreno*

Tank and his dad, an American Hero. *Kristi Moreno*

two children who are shaping up to be just like their daddy. She has friends and family who love Nick and will gladly share a drink and a story anytime. He will be a part of them forever.

She's glad they made the most of their too-brief time together. His death brought few regrets in how they lived their lives. They said the things that needed to be said and did the things they needed to do, never taking their love or their time together for granted. They lived life to the fullest.

Reflecting on Nick and their romance, she says with a smile, "Even knowing how our story ends, I wouldn't change a thing. I'll keep my five minutes because even though it wasn't long enough together, it was long enough to last forever."

Christmas at Arlington. *Tasha Sprovtsoff*

Staff Sergeant Justin Schmalstieg on deployment. *Ann Schmalstieg*

☆ ☆ ☆

HER FAITH AND HER ART

Ann Schmalstieg

On Monday Ann Schmalstieg finished her written thesis and was looking forward to getting back to her art. She missed the moments expressing herself on canvas rather than in words. She was an artist, not a writer, and with the hint of a smile says, "I hate using words." She spent most of Tuesday working on *Agape*. There was a sense of sorrow in the charcoal on paper, something she didn't initially intend. Despite a strong faith in God, fear nagged at her soul with Justin in Afghanistan, and the emotion carried over into her work.

It was nine and she was just about to sit down to a late dinner when there was a knock at the door. No one ever came at this hour and she was curious yet cautious of the intrusion. Peering out the window, she saw three men in uniform: a Navy chaplain and two Marines. She knew immediately!

Ann and Justin before his final deployment. *Ann Schmalstieg*

☆ ☆ ☆

Top: Justin and his family at his graduation from EOD school. *Ann Schmalstieg*
Bottom: Iraq 2006 after the vehicle was hit by an IED. *Bryan Carter*

In Iraq holding a 155mm artillery shell made in South Africa and found in an IED. *Bryan Carter*

Ann is presented with the flag that draped Justin's casket as he was laid to rest. *Ann Schmalstieg*

Although her heart remains shattered, for those who know Ann, they know her faith and her art have allowed her to cope with the devastating loss.

In Justin, she found not only a husband but her spiritual partner: sharing a prayer life, reading the Bible, and saying the rosary.

Sunrises held a special meaning. Ann tried to train herself to paint quickly by capturing the ever-changing hues of the sunrise. She told Justin of her love for the early hours. The morning after they were married, he woke her to watch the sunrise together, a gesture of love that still brings a tear. The day he deployed, as they waited for the bureaucracy to catch up with the mission, Justin pointed out the sunrise, bringing a sense of peace, counteracting the unknown the future held. Then the morning after she received the news of Justin's death she arose early, sleep not coming easily. As she walked out into the yard, a thick, overcast sky hid the sun. It still came up; she just couldn't see it. It was as if God were protecting her, not wanting to spoil all the beautiful sunrises she shared with her husband.

She knows now their lives were much like those early mornings. The colors they shared in sunrises and in life were all too brief.

☆ ☆ ☆

Ann likes the way art allows one to express aspects of experience without putting them into words. You can scream without screaming, giving a visual voice to the hurt and devastation. Words can define objects but not always the emotions engulfed in reality. Another Gold Star wife offered the highest compliment on a piece she purchased from Ann. The wife "understood" what Ann was saying in her work . . . words without speaking.

☆ ☆ ☆

That first Sunday after Justin's death, Ann went to church. The beauty of the Mass took her from where she was, the sorrow and numbness temporarily dissipating as she realized she could still perceive the beauty in life. She realized she was not alone. "Mary had to watch her own son's death on the cross. Now I understand how the crucifix can be viewed as an image of love."

Ann and Justin. *Ann Schmalstieg*

Top row from left to right: Slowly; EOD Memorial; Middle row from left to right: Hand Study; Holding Together; Placed; Bottom row: Sacrifice: Major and Minor All by Ann Schmalstieg

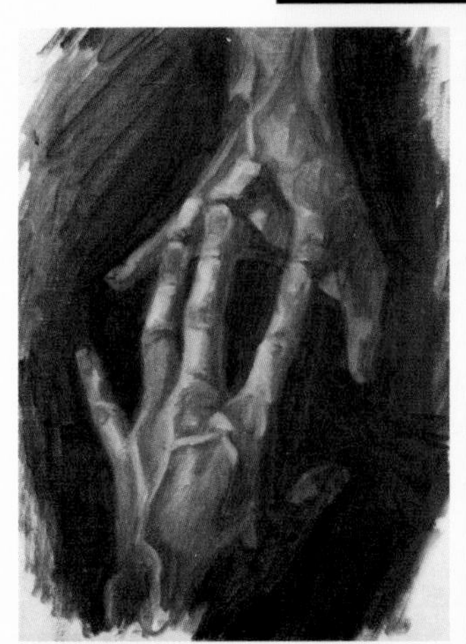

3

★ ★ ★

EVEN WHEN HE WASN'T SO EASY TO LOVE

Lindsey and Trey Humphrey

The morning fog hung heavy in the northernmost section of Camp Pendleton, home to the 5th Marine Regiment. The Marines from Kilo Company stood at attention as Lieutenant Colonel Christeon C. Griffin pinned the Bronze Star with Combat V for valor on Marine Corps Sergeant Thomas B. Humphrey III, known to his friends as Trey. The actions for which Trey was being honored took place sixteen months earlier and many in the formation were new to the unit, not even part of the Marine Corps when 3rd Battalion, 5th Marines last deployed to Afghanistan. All, however, knew they were in the presence of American heroes, members of 3/5 who distinguished themselves in combat, paying a tremendous price in the name of freedom.

Trey Humphrey after being awarded the Bronze Star with Combat V for valor. *Bob Hamer*

Trey stood shoulder to shoulder with those who fought with

him in Iraq and Afghanistan. There was the cane and a slight limp but few knew he was missing his right leg and fighting to save his left. Nor did they know he had "died" twice while being medically evacuated from the battlefield. They just knew he exhibited extraordinary heroism half a world away.

Being in the company of the men with whom he served made the morning very special, but the nagging uncertainty about his future clouded the event. It was more than the missing limb; the IED had ruptured his identity. He loved being a Marine and he would never again lead men into battle.

In essence the Bronze Star, the same medal his grandfather was awarded for actions in World War II, marked the end of the Marine Corps career he valued. The sacrifices he made to wear the title "Marine" would now be stories for a backyard barbecue sometime in the future, somewhere beyond the confines of a military base.

* * *

If you saw her sitting at an outdoor café in Beverly Hills you would assume she's a Tinseltown starlet, but Lindsey Humphrey is no celebrity; she's a hero. There's a difference, even if too few people understand the distinction. Like the Marines who carried Trey's fractured body to safety, she remained by his side through the surgeries and rehabilitation even when he wasn't so easy to love.

Sergeant Trey Humphrey and Lindsey at the Marine Corps Birthday Ball. *Lindsey Humphrey*

Although they both attended Foothill High School in Henderson, Nevada, just south of Las Vegas, and she admits to having a schoolgirl crush on the popular senior three-sport athlete, Trey paid little attention to the skinny blond freshman. In a few years that would change but not before Trey left for the University of Nevada, Reno, with plans to pursue a degree in business and gaming management. Though he stayed several years his heart was never in his studies. He was treading water. Aimlessly flapping his arms staying afloat made little sense. Without telling anyone of his decision until after he signed the enlistment papers, he joined the Marine Corps.

Trey on combat patrol. *Trey Humphrey*

Top: In Iraq with Private First Class Nakai Sinohui. *Trey Humphrey.*
Bottom: Trey: a protector of Muslim children. *Trey Humphrey*

He excelled at boot camp; motivated and focused. At twenty-two Trey was older than most, the recruit series honor graduate, and the company high scorer at the rifle range. When he pinned on the Eagle, Globe, and Anchor he was a private first class and reported to the School of Infantry, where he continued to excel, graduating as a lance corporal. Within two months of reporting to the battalion, he deployed to Iraq for the first of three combat deployments. Less than three weeks in-country he saw the war up close and personal, earning the coveted Combat Action Ribbon. The boredom of the classroom less than a year earlier was a distant memory. He found his calling. He was a Marine!

* * *

With the War on Terror in full battle mode, the training never stopped. As soon as the men returned from one deployment, they began preparing for the next. To cope with the stress of war and the intense training leading up to combat, Trey and his Marine friends often traveled to Las Vegas on weekend liberty. It was during these frequent weekend get-togethers with high school friends the battle-tested Marine began to take notice of Lindsey, no longer a skinny freshman.

She obviously knew Trey was a Marine when they began dating and despite warnings from her father, who had served in the Navy, she was falling in love. Within weeks of their first date, Trey left for his second deployment to Iraq and they began a long-distance romance, exchanging letters and the occasional phone call.

Upon his return the relationship was in full bloom, though still somewhat distant with Lindsey in Las Vegas pursuing a career in banking and Trey stationed at Camp Pendleton, in Southern California. Once again the Marine Corps put more distance between them when he left in January 2009 for a seven-month deployment to the Pacific, training with Australian and Philippine troops.

Trey returned in September, and on New Year's Day 2010, during a visit to Lake Tahoe, Trey proposed. She said yes without hesitating.

The initial excitement of the engagement dimmed when three weeks later his battalion announced it was being deployed to Afghanistan in September. Lindsey was getting a pretty good look at what life was like in the Marine Corps . . . four seven-month deployments in four years.

She didn't want to rush the wedding, so she and Trey decided to wait until he returned from the latest deployment, which would be May 2011. Since she wanted an outdoor wedding in Las Vegas, the summer months were out. Looking over the calendar, they realized September 10,

Trey proposing to Lindsey at Lake Tahoe. *Lindsey Humphrey*

2011—or 9/10/11—was a Saturday. Trey assumed he would never forget the unique date, so they booked the wedding eighteen months in advance!

☆ ☆ ☆

On September 26, 2010, 3rd Battalion, 5th Marines, nicknamed Darkhorse, deployed to Afghanistan. During the seven-month deployment the unit would sustain the highest casualty rate of any Marine Corps battalion in the decade-long War on Terror.

Inside an armored vehicle. *Trey Humphrey*

Assigned to Forward Operating Base Inkerman, in the upper Sangin Valley, within the first month Trey led his squad on twenty extended combat patrols, eighteen of which resulted in decisive engagements with insurgent forces.

November 8 marked a notable encounter. At 3 A.M., reinforced with snipers and a machine gunner, his squad headed out in the early morning darkness. Although the black of night added to the danger of missing the more obvious signs of recently planted

A Marine patrol outside FOB Inkerman. *USMC Cpl. Benjamin Crilly*

IEDs, the combat-experienced warriors took a less traveled route to their planned destination.

The Marines noted in previous patrols the insurgents would follow in trace. The plan this morning was to set an ambush in the early morning hours. When a second Marine squad, led by Sergeant Jonathan Decker, walked through the kill zone, Trey's squad would be ready for the trailing Taliban.

On patrol through a cornfield where visibility is next to zero. *USMC Sgt. Mark Fayloga*

Cornfields covered the irrigated land. As harvest neared the stalks were as tall as the Marines. Trey positioned his men before the sun rose, prepared to engage the enemy.

Before Sergeant Decker's squad could make its way to the kill zone, they were met with harassing fire and the ambush plans collapsed. The five or six hours Trey's men had been waiting patiently in an Afghani cornfield were wasted. Trey ordered his men to break down the ambush and return to base, following Decker's squad, which was also returning to the base.

The Marines refer to them as "scan eagles," the unmanned aerial vehicles that patrol the skies seeking insurgent activity on the ground. As Trey and his men were heading home, radio traffic

A Scan Eagle UAV: the "eyes" for a Marine patrol on the ground. *USMC Cpl. Samantha H. Arrington*

reported the scan eagle spotted a half-dozen fully armed Taliban several hundred yards west of their location. Within a short period of time the Marines began receiving inaccurate automatic weapon fire, a trick the terrorists used, hoping to force the Marines to respond and thus identify their position. The mature cornfield made it impossible for the Marines to see the insurgents who were also patrolling in the blind.

The UAV then observed the Taliban entering a building known to Trey and his men. The Command Center ordered Sergeant Decker's squad to investigate the building and for Trey's squad, which had been out for almost eight hours, to return to the patrol base. But Trey's squad was reinforced with snipers and a machine gun. Decker's was not. One secret to military success is overwhelming firepower. Trey wasn't about to let Decker's squad go it alone. The need for military superiority required his squad to assist and he convinced the COC to allow his men to remain outside the wire.

A canal ran west into the area where the building was located. Canals were often the safest route because it was difficult to plant IEDs in water, but they did bring the added danger of forcing the men to walk the "fatal funnel."

The sun was nearing its peak, with only a few soft clouds in the late morning sky. The men were hot and the cool water of the canal, although filthy, provided some relief from the Afghanistan heat.

The two squads proceeded west up the canal, sometimes encountering chest-high water. It was wet, sloppy, and soggy but at least in the short term provided the safest and quickest route to the house where the Taliban awaited.

About two klicks up the canal Trey encountered gunfire from two or three Taliban, their rounds splashing in the water in front of him. Trey quickly responded, returning fire, watching an insurgent die from a well-placed head shot. The smell of gunpowder hung in the air as the squad continued the forward approach toward a cluster of compounds. As they neared, the gunfire ceased. There was almost an eerie silence. Then as the lead element climbed out of the water, firing erupted from a large walled compound.

The Taliban opened up with everything they had, spraying enfilade fire straight down the canal, the Marines now in a perfect kill zone. Both squads raced to the banks of the canal seeking cover but returning fire. One Marine was hit immediately, taking a round to the thigh. He needed medical aid. Doc Collins and Doc Long, Navy corpsmen, raced through the fusillade of gunfire to the downed Marine, assessing the injury and providing aid while all three were still in the water. Trey maneuvered his men, moving too quickly to do a proper sweep of the area for IEDs,

A Marine patrol along a Sangin District irrigation canal. *USMC Sgt. Logan Pierce*

laying down a base of fire, spraying the area with all they had. A running gun battle ensued as the Marines killed numerous Taliban but suffered no further losses, at least on this patrol.

As Lieutenant General T. D. Waldhauser said in the Bronze Star commendation, throughout the deployment Trey "displayed unparalleled tactical skill by maneuvering his squad on enemy positions and coordinating an untold number of indirect fire as well as close air support." The citation went on to describe the events of November 8: "[D]uring tactical site exploitation of a compound, his squad came under heavy enemy Rocket Propelled Grenades, small arms, and machinegun fire. While under fire and with complete disregard for his own safety, he moved into an open danger area to identify the enemy's positions, establish a base of fire, and direct his maneuver elements in a flanking attack that ultimately destroyed the enemy."

⋆ ⋆ ⋆

Lindsey remained in Las Vegas, employed at the Bank of America in nearby Boulder City. With Trey deployed, she was putting in ten-hour days as the assistant bank manager, planning a wedding, and keeping busy with family and friends.

Unless he was on a mission, Trey called every Monday morning. She would arrive at the bank early and take the call in a back office where she could monitor the security cameras as the employees arrived. On November 8, following the gun battle with the Taliban, Trey called. It was their longest call, thirty-one minutes. As they hung up, each said, "I love you," and Lindsey ended with "Be safe." Trey responded, "I still have ten fingers and ten toes." All that was about to change.

⋆ ⋆ ⋆

November 9 was supposed to be a down day for the squad; no patrols, no working parties. But Trey had a hard time standing down. It wasn't in his nature to kick back when Marines were in harm's way. By midmorning he was in the Combat Operations Center, "battle-tracking": listening to the radio, marking the map, viewing the monitor of the coverage from the UAV flying overhead. Sergeant Iwatsuru's squad was on patrol in an area laden with roadside bombs.

The FOB was located on the high ground overlooking much of the valley. From the base you could often hear the IEDs detonating but Trey didn't hear the blast that interrupted the relative calm of the morning. He did hear the radio traffic that barked, "Michaels is down" followed

The irrigation ditches in Afghanistan also double as the local sewers. *USMC Sgt. Logan Pierce*

by the nine-line medevac order. Sergeant Scott Michaels, the machine-gun squad leader, had stepped on a low-grade IED. He'd shattered his foot and needed evacuation.

Because Sergeant Michaels had not lost his foot—at least not yet: he would later have the foot amputated—the Marines didn't want to risk sending a helicopter into a potentially "hot LZ" to pick up a "non-critical" Marine casualty who could be moved to a safer location. The injury was not life-or-death and time was not of the essence. But the squad came under harassing fire and was having difficulty extricating the wounded Marine. Four Marines loaded Michaels on a poncho litter and were struggling to get him off the battlefield. They needed help and without hesitation, Trey sprang into action.

Within minutes Trey gathered his men, including the platoon commander, Second Lieutenant Tom Schueman, and the platoon sergeant, Staff Sergeant Tim Hendley. A sniper or two joined, as did Corporal Mike Spivy, a combat engineer. Approximately fifteen Marines prepared to link up with the other squad and help rescue the downed Marine.

The firefight was about two kilometers from the FOB. Trey's plan was to move as quickly as feasible about a thousand meters, hopeful if the insurgents saw the squad-size formation moving toward the battle site they might break contact. If they didn't run, Trey and his men were prepared to engage and neutralize the threat.

It appeared a few insurgents were making the extrication of Sergeant Michaels difficult. Trey and his Marines took a fairly direct route to the engagement. His men were seasoned fighters who knew enough to stay off the popular trails. The men demonstrated in the past they had "good eyes." They could spot potential trouble areas. They knew to steer clear of fresh mounds of dirt. Any troubling sites would be swept by Mike Spivy, the combat engineer who would survive this patrol but before the end of the year lose his arm in a blast while working with another squad. Trey's men visually linked up with the other squad and provided a shield as the wounded Marine was safely rescued.

The men had moved out about fifteen hundred meters and failed to find the enemy. The firefight seemed over. Radio traffic now reported Sergeant Michaels was safe at the base, so Trey gave his men the order to return. The mission was complete; the injured Marine extricated from the battlefield. The squad slowly made their way toward the FOB, the three fire teams somewhat spread out across the open field. Within seconds gunfire broke out and a larger firefight ensued. One of Trey's fire teams, the one to the rear of the loose formation, was pinned down by the insurgent's assault, an enemy machine gun spraying the landscape with death.

Unable to make contact with the pinned-down fire team leader, Trey turned to Lieutenant Schueman. The platoon commander okayed Trey's plan to have another fire team lay down a

Top: Marine armored vehicles on patrol. *USMC Cpl. Meghan Gonzales*
Bottom: Army "Dustoff" HH-60 evacuating a Marine casualty. *USMC Cpl. Bryan Nygaard*

base of fire, killing the enemy machine gunners or at least distracting them so the pinned-down fire team could escape. Trey turned, preparing to link up with his nearest fire team. He took two or three steps. There was a click, a boom, then smoke, debris, and chaos.

Trey was at the center of the explosion. He'd stepped on a pressure-plate IED and was blown high into the air. Despite the bedlam he remained calm; panic was not in his makeup, and composure prevailed. He could see nothing through the sweat, sand, and the grit engulfing him but his world was now in slow motion; his only concern his men. Was anyone else injured in the blast?

When Trey landed he was facedown in the depression created by the explosion. Corporal Matt Bland rushed to Trey's rescue, pulling him from the crater. Doc Collins also raced to the explosion site.

The right leg below the knee was eviscerated and the left leg badly damaged. On multiple occasions during his deployments Trey applied tourniquets to save the lives of wounded Marines. Now others were performing the task he practiced frequently and applied too often. To prevent exsanguination the men strapped a lightweight tourniquet on the right leg, adjusted the strap by pulling it through the clip, ratcheting it tight, then screwing down the small pin.

Monitoring the radio traffic in the COC, Gunny Carlisle knew what was happening and knew his Marines needed help. He sprinted to an MRAP (a Mine Resistant Ambush Protected armored fighting vehicle) parked near the COC. The gunny, Corporal Warner, and Navy corpsman Bob "Doc" Blehm raced about five hundred meters to meet the men carrying Trey. They loaded his wounded body and hurried back to the FOB. The shooting didn't stop, however, as Trey heard rounds pinging off the vehicle. He remained conscious throughout the trip, repeatedly asking for water but getting none.

Once he arrived at the battalion aid station, he was hit with morphine. He was loaded on the helicopter and during takeoff saw a large needle being plunged into his thigh. His life flickered. He had not yet escaped death. Twice his heart stopped on the chopper ride off the battlefield. He remained unconscious on the C-17 "Nightingale" flights all the way from Afghanistan to the Regional Medical Center Landstuhl, Germany, and eventually to the medical center in Bethesda, Maryland, where he awoke weeks later.

☆ ☆ ☆

November 9 began as a routine day for Lindsey. She proudly supported Trey, frequently mailing boxes filled with his favorites, bringing some of the comforts of home to the battlefield. Over the weekend she prepared a Thanksgiving gift pack with two logs of Grizzly Wintergreen tobacco,

The care package Lindsey prepared for Trey the weekend before he was wounded. *Lindsey Humphrey*

astronaut freeze-dried ice cream, candies, some pictures of her with friends, and deodorant, always a welcome item in third-world Afghanistan. With artistic flair she decorated the outside in puffy paint, marking one side with "310 days to our wedding."

Work was slow. As the lunch hour neared she called her mom, Bobbie, a flight attendant who was between flights, to see if she wanted to meet for lunch. Lindsey thought her mom was acting strange on the phone but dismissed it, quickly calling a friend, who agreed to meet. Mary Ann wanted to show off her new BMW and hurried to the bank.

Lindsey was only a bite into the lunch special when she received a text message from Alex, the daughter of her mom's best friend, Marie. The message read "U r in my prayers Lindsey." She froze momentarily before reading the text again. She wasn't sure what the text meant but sensed something was wrong, her mind traveling back to the phone call with her mother less than an hour earlier.

Immediate calls to her mother and Trey's parents went unanswered. When she called home her brother Eric's response, "I don't know," wasn't convincing.

Still at the restaurant, a second text from her cousin Tiffany came across her phone: "I just heard about Trey. I'm so sorry. If you need anything I'm here for you." Now she was in full panic mode. Lindsey called Marie, whose daughter sent the initial text. At first Marie was reluctant to talk, knowing Bobbie and Trey's parents were en route, but with Lindsey in tears, Marie relented and said, "He's alive."

"Don't lie," said Lindsey.

Marie responded, "I wouldn't lie but Trey's been seriously injured."

Mary Ann rushed Lindsey back to the bank a half mile from the restaurant. When they pulled into the parking lot, Lindsey spotted Trey's dad, Tom, sitting alone in his car. Trey's mom and Lindsey's mom were in the bank hoping to find Lindsey. Her eyes filled with tears and her heart pounded as she jumped from Mary Ann's BMW and rushed to Tom. When he explained the phone call he had received earlier in the morning, Lindsey collapsed in his arms, her emotions surrendering to the news.

The casualty report delivered over the phone stated Trey's right foot was gone, and that there were wounds to his left thigh, a broken left upper arm, and shrapnel wounds throughout his body.

★ ★ ★

An agonizing week later, Lindsey, Tom, and Trey's mother, Robin, left on a D.C.-bound red-eye Sunday night, landing Monday morning.

Upon arrival at Bethesda they went to the Marine Corps Liaison Office, where Staff Sergeant Marzelli provided an update and tried to prepare them for what they would soon experience. The briefing took about thirty minutes but seemed like forever. Lindsey wasn't interested in policy and procedure. She wanted to see the man she loved.

Once upstairs at the intensive care unit, they were held up again as the sheets were being changed in Trey's room. The anticipation had been building for a week, apprehension consuming her every thought. Now Lindsey was a few feet from seeing the man she loved unconditionally, but first another delay. The family was required to "glove and gown up" before entering the room.

Lindsey was the first to enter . . . Trey looked dead! He was pale, gaunt, and motionless, in a medically induced coma. Metal and machines were everywhere. Tubes ran from his mouth and nose. His neck was braced and his hand encased in what appeared to be a large cheese block, a blanket covering his legs. She was crushed by the sight and fought to contain her emotions.

Lindsey kept waiting for him to say, "Hey, babe," but there was nothing. No response, no recognition. The family stood in quiet shock, holding back tears. A mother and father viewed their son as they had never seen him. His body riddled with wounds. A fiancée saw the man of strength she hoped to marry in a state of total physical submission. He looked helpless and they

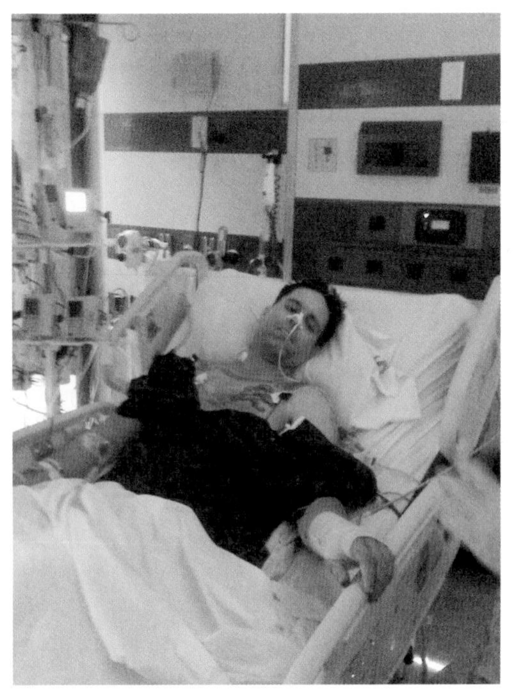

Trey as Lindsey first saw him after he was wounded. *Lindsey Humphrey*

questioned whether only the machines of modern medicine were keeping him alive.

The nurse went over the extent of his injuries . . . head to toe, or at least so they thought. When she peeled back a portion of the blanket, they saw the right leg was missing below the knee. There was no discoloration to the toes on his left foot, which peeked out beneath the blanket, and there was no mention of a situation requiring a decision in a few days that continues to haunt the family.

Now that Trey was safely in the United States, the doctors agreed to ease him out of the coma. As the medication wore off, Trey took on a zombie-like appearance. His eyes would open and just as quickly close. When he reopened his eyes, he'd stare at the family, his eyes floating in a vacuum of uncertainty. He still wasn't speaking and appeared confused by his surroundings and circumstances.

Without warning Trey would flail his arms as if in a rage, throw off the cheese block, and then abruptly all motion would subside. The doctors described this as his brain trying to exercise that portion of his body it could still control.

Waiting for the words "I love you" or "Hi, babe," Lindsey remained by his side. Trey's confused state persisted and the first thing he uttered after coming out of the coma was far from romantic, as he mumbled, "Soda." The nurse brought him ginger ale, his favorite drink, but it was Shasta ginger ale. Trey muttered, "Canada Dry," and when she informed him the hospital had only Shasta he replied out of the side of his mouth, "This is ridiculous."

Lindsey had yet to hear the words she longed to hear and wanted so much for him to reassure her. Her emotional reserves were nearing empty. It was difficult to smile and she couldn't fake happiness with the anxiety her soul was experiencing.

Trey had difficulty coming to grips with the situation. His behavior was bizarre and beyond what the family ever witnessed. Throughout the day the nurses would remind him he was in Maryland, not Afghanistan, where he continued to think he was still serving.

Continuing his questionable behavior, he once demanded of Lindsey, "Why are you here? You're intruding. I'm working."

When Lindsey mentioned they were going to be married, his response shocked her to tears: "I'm already married. I married an Afghan woman but I divorced her because she was a bitch."

As they later learned, during the time in the medically induced coma, Trey's dreams became real, at least to him, and it wasn't until the medication wore off that he was able to separate reality from the hallucinations of his mind.

Lindsey with Trey just days after he was wounded, a moment Trey doesn't remember. *Lindsey Humphrey*

* * *

Tom's cousin Barbie Covey, a medical doctor, came to Bethesda. Though the staff tried to be informative there was just too much being thrown at the family and Tom wanted someone who could interpret the medical-speak. Her input was valuable as the family faced some difficult decisions.

On Thursday, the third day Lindsey and the family were in Maryland, she wanted some alone time with Trey and awoke early. She did her hair and makeup, looking like a Hollywood ingénue strolling down Beverly Hills' Rodeo Drive, and took the shuttle from the Marriott to the Metro and then to the hospital. She was excited to spend a few minutes with the man she loved before family and the constant barrage of medical personnel crowded into the room.

Before entering she did one more quick check of the mirror, threw on the plastic yellow hospital gown, donned the latex gloves, and prepared to spend time with the man of her dreams. As she entered the room expecting to hear, "Good morning, babe" she was greeted by a deep guttural laugh. Trey's eyes were glued to the TV set: Jerry Springer! He didn't even look up and his only response was a mumbled "I like drama and black people."

Lindsey was crushed. She was pouring every ounce of emotional energy into Trey's well-being and her reward was a fiancé who didn't seem to care. Her heart ached as she questioned what happened to the man she knew prior to this deployment.

At one point, Trey, still confused, asked Lindsey why she was there, thinking he was still in Afghanistan. "It's so dangerous over here."

Lindsey was no medical professional but she knew things weren't right. He mumbled, he refused to open his mouth, and his erratic behavior was beyond what she was seeing of other combat-wounded patients on the floor. When she made her concerns known to a nurse, a speech therapist was ordered.

The therapist performed a variety of tests and commented that his throat wasn't functioning properly, but suggested that wasn't abnormal for a person with a "broken jaw." Lindsey and the family members looked at each other in shock. No one told them Trey had a broken jaw.

In the waiting room the tears came as guilt overcame her. Lindsey yelled at Trey for not opening his mouth and now she learned why. He couldn't. His jaw was shattered. Not only was he in pain but mechanically the jaw couldn't perform. Even in his previous surgeries the operating room personnel had complained Trey wasn't cooperating, refusing to open his mouth so he could be ventilated. It was truly a medical disconnect, as not everyone was aware of the full extent of his injuries.

With this information now known to everyone, a feeding tube was inserted.

Lindsey cried when Trey succeeded in getting a straw to his mouth for a sip of water. *Lindsey Humphrey*

The next day the maxillofacial surgeons examined Trey, attempting to figure out a plan for the badly damaged jaw. There was the initial fear of cutting nerves if they went in for reconstructive surgery. Wiring the jaw shut, allowing it to heal, was out of the question because Trey was averaging three surgeries a week, each requiring he be ventilated with a tube during the procedure. A decision was made to attempt the risky reconstructive surgery, implanting screws and a plate on the left side of his jaw and a plate on the right.

Trey was still struggling to take sips of water without assistance and spent one morning trying to move the straw to his mouth. Lindsey could only watch, her heart aching as she watched the determination of a combat hero attempting to perform such a simple task. When she returned in the afternoon she was greeted by "Hey, babe, guess what I learned to do." For the next fifteen minutes, Trey slowly and cautiously lifted the cup as the straw touched his lips and he took a sip. For the first time in Trey's presence, the tears flowed; tears of joy celebrating a task everyone takes for granted.

For a reason known only to the medicated Trey, since he still can't recall his frustration, he was upset with a particular nurse and vocalized it, often in a loud, embarrassing fashion. He was convinced the nurse was laughing at him with others in the hallway. The shift change occurred at 1900 hours, 7:00 P.M. civilian time. One evening Trey confided in Lindsey, "Shift change is at nineteen hundred and I'm throwing her overboard." Fortunately for the nurse, Trey was hooked up to too many machines to make his way to the starboard side of his imaginary ship.

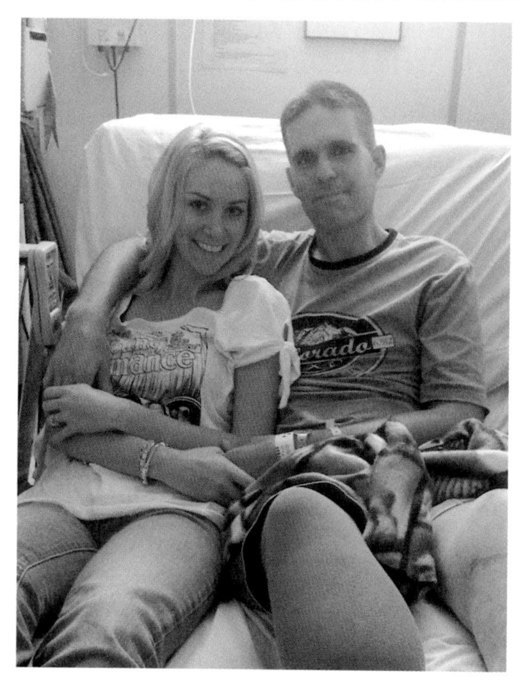

Progress. *Lindsey Humphrey*

Trey had been out of the coma for almost a week and was still unaware his right leg below the knee had been traumatically amputated in the explosion. Lindsey was also unaware of the full extent of his injuries. She was shocked when the first weekend in Bethesda passed without much fanfare and she was greeted Monday morning with the news the doctors were contemplating amputating the left leg!

She had spent days and nights with Trey. She watched medical personnel come and go, treating what remained of his right leg. Three times since the family's arrival at Bethesda Trey had been wheeled to surgery for treatment to the nub of his right leg. The toes of his left foot often slipped above the blanket and no imperfections were evident. There was no bruising, no scarring. What could possibly be wrong with his left leg?

The news of possible amputation brought home the reality . . . his left leg had been severely damaged. Between the knee and the ankle all that remained was essentially the tibia and fibula, the bones of the lower leg. The area was devoid of muscle and tissue.

The doctors provided Trey's parents with their assessment, leaving the amputation decision to Tom and Robin since Trey was still not fully coherent. Though Lindsey was not legally part of the decision-making process because she and Trey weren't married, the Humphreys included her in this life-altering choice. Tom's cousin Barbie provided input and concurred with the doctors' recommendation of amputation.

The ten-hour surgery was scheduled and would include closing up the stump on his right leg, reconstructing the jaw, and amputating the left leg below the knee. Rather than wait around at the hospital the family returned to the hotel. Within hours the hospital called saying there were "issues." Lindsey feared the worst, frightened Trey had died in surgery.

They rushed back to the hospital and learned when doctors removed the bandages surrounding the wound, they could smell the infection and a quick examination confirmed the initial assessment. The left leg was too infected for them to operate.

Trey was placed immediately on antibiotics with plans to remove the leg the next week.

During this time frame Trey became more coherent. He learned he lost his right leg and his dad told him of the decision to amputate the left. For the first time Lindsey saw the full extent of the damage to the left leg . . . bone and little else between the knee and the foot; only two of five nerves functioning.

As the massive doses of antibiotics fought the infection, Trey was now participating in the medical decisions. He chose to try to save his leg, and two miracle men entered the picture: Navy doctors Patrick Basile and Ian Valerio, both plastic surgeons willing to salvage the leg with an experimental procedure.

In what seems like something from the imagination of a sci-fi screenwriter, doctors removed an eighteen-inch strip of trapezius muscle from the left side of Trey's back and attached it to insertion points below the knee and at the foot. The ten-hour procedure was believed to be a success. Prayers were offered and fingers crossed; there was always the chance of the body rejecting the new muscle but the doctors were confident they had succeeded in salvaging the leg.

* * *

As Trey recovered from the experimental surgery, the medical staff was able to isolate the cause of his erratic behavior. His temperamental periodic outbursts had chased Lindsey out of the room in tears, vowing never to return, but long talks with her mom, still in Las Vegas, even chats with the hospital chaplains brought about a peace that helped her weather the storm. It turned out Trey had a strong sensitivity to Dilaudid, a potent, morphine-derivative pain reliever, which had resulted in his near-psychotic conduct. Once off the medication his behavior normalized.

As Christmas approached, they knew they would be spending the holidays at Bethesda. Lindsey took the initiative. She wasn't about to let the clouds of doubt and desperation darken

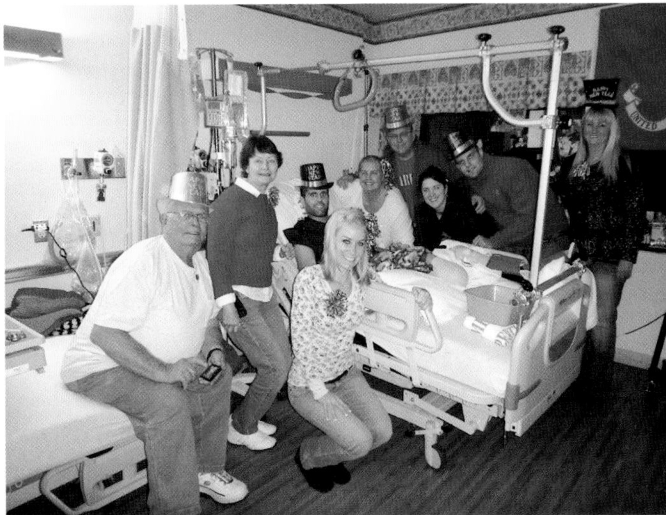

Lindsey decorated Trey's room at Bethesda for Christmas and with hopes for a better New Year. *Lindsey Humphrey*

the holidays. Using dental floss, she hung ornaments throughout the room. Lights were strung from the ceiling and bows taped to the walls. A Marine Corps T-shirt and panties provided wall decorations, as did a T-shirt from the Las Vegas Fire Department. A Marine Corps flag autographed by every visitor hung on one of the walls. On the door Lindsey displayed family pictures, Christmas cards, even a letter to Santa. Blown-up surgical gloves decorated a tree. Others on the floor followed suit and soon the rooms displayed the sights of the season.

But Christmas Day is one she won't forget and hopes to never relive. Christmas was a big

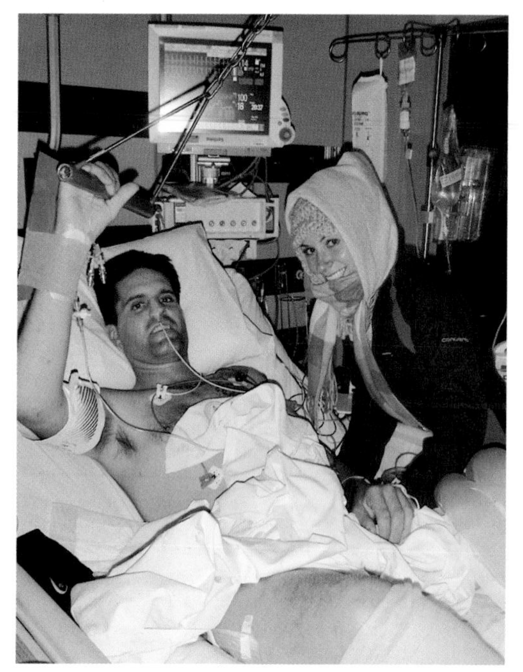

Trey's Christmas gift at Bethesda: a transfusion. *Lindsey Humphrey*

day in Lindsey's family and she was homesick for her mom and the relatives who usually crowded into their home. Trey wanted the day to be special and provided a list to his dad for presents he and Santa would give, hoping for as normal a Christmas as possible. But the day didn't begin with a visit from Kris Kringle. On Christmas morning it was determined Trey needed two pints of blood, the result of too many surgeries and his body not reproducing blood cells at a sufficient pace.

As the nurse prepped him for the transfusion, the stent near his wrist wasn't cooperating. It was decided to infuse the blood in the upper arm. As the transfusion began, Trey kept saying something wasn't right. No one wanted to listen. As his complaints continued, they realized the needle had missed the vein and the blood was being pumped directly into the muscle. His bicep was full of blood, ballooning underneath the skin, taking hours to dissipate. Trey fought to keep his sanity through the barely tolerable pain of the procedure. A sedative knocked him out for the day as the opening of presents and any attempts at celebrating the holiday were put off until eight that evening . . . not a Christmas to remember.

Lance Corporal James Boelk, USMC, KIA Afghanistan. *Boelk Family*

The catastrophic injuries to members of 3rd Battalion, 5th Marines continued. In the early weeks of the mission in Sangin, two Marines who paid the ultimate sacrifice were Second Lieutenant Robert Michael Kelly and Lance Corporal James Boelk.

Boelk was the first member of the battalion killed and Kelly's father is General John F. Kelly, one of the most respected members of the Marine Corps family. Each must grieve in his own way but Trey and Lindsey

Lance Corporal James Boelk laid to rest at Quantico National Cemetery. *Boelk Family*

could only marvel at the Kelly and Boelk families. General Kelly and his family frequently visited the wounded at Bethesda. The general did this not to check off the box as part of some management-leadership requirement but in genuine love for the men who served in the arena with his son. The Boelk family was an amazing testament to faith, visiting the wounded at Bethesda several times a week, bringing homemade cookies, even fresh fruit smoothies, since Trey's broken jaw prevented him from eating solid foods. When most would prefer to grieve in a quiet corner and not be reminded of the tragedy that took a son's life, the Kelly and Boelk families provided new meaning to the motto *Semper Fi* . . . always faithful.

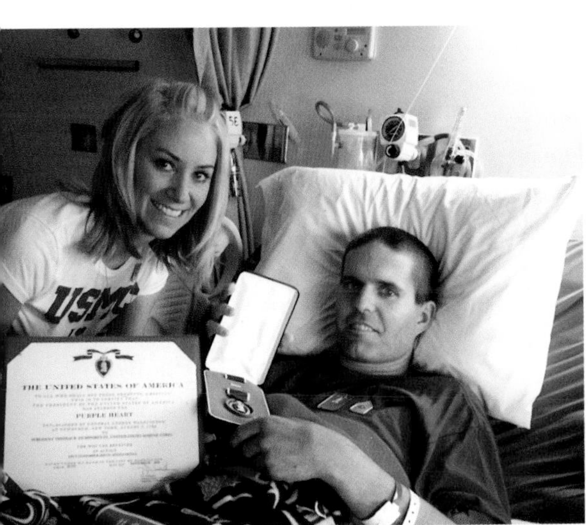

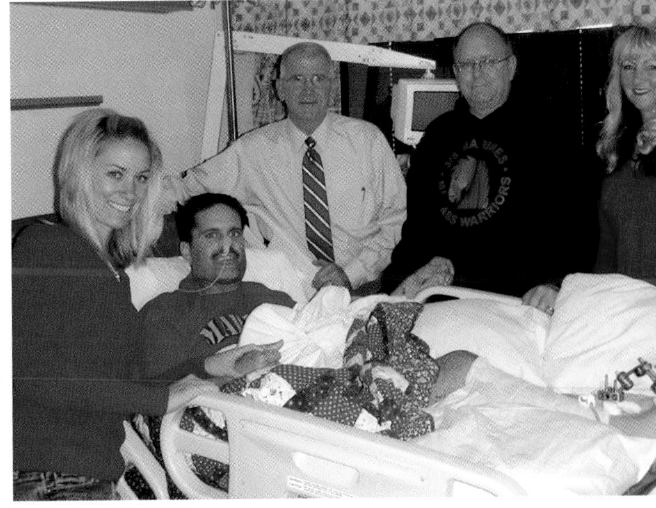

Left: Trey receives his Purple Heart. Lindsey holding the citation. *Lindsey Humphrey. Right:* When I visited Trey at Bethesda he was much improved, as evidenced by the smiles. *Lindsey Humphrey*

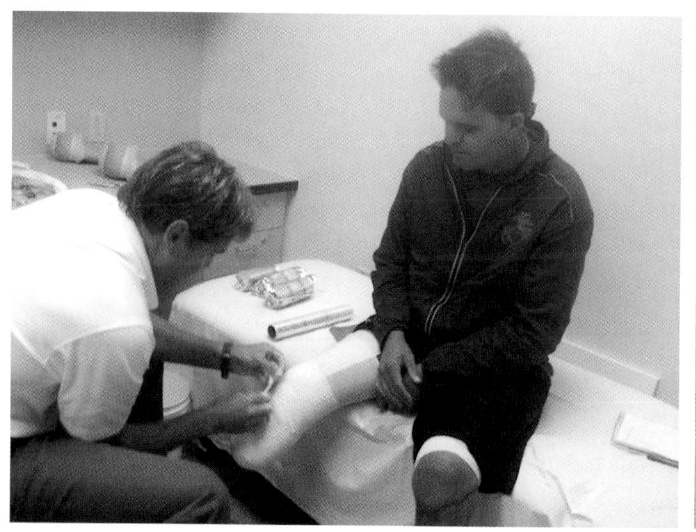

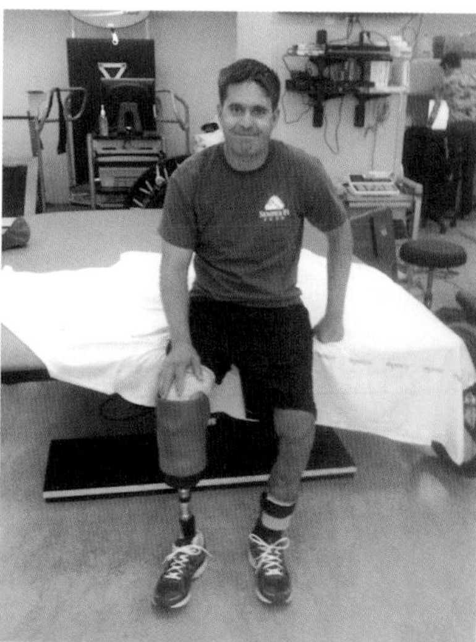

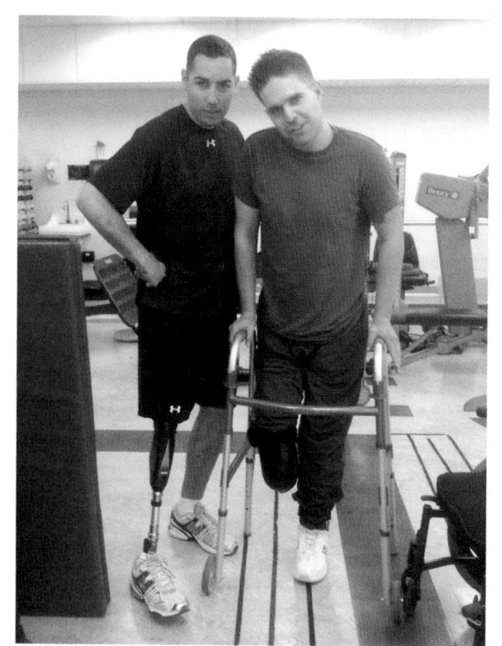

Top left: Trey being fitted for his prosthetics. *Lindsey Humphrey. Top right:* Trey's new leg. *Lindsey Humphrey. Bottom left:* With First Lieutenant Cameron West, USMC, in physical therapy. *Lindsey Humphrey. Bottom right:* The brotherhood of Marines. *Lindsey Humphrey*

Left: Lindsey and Trey at a San Diego Padres game. *Lindsey Humphrey.* *Right:* Two heroes with matching legs. *Lindsey Humphrey*

Trey at the memorial service for the Marines of 3/5 who made the ultimate sacrifice. *Lindsey Humphrey*

During the stay at Bethesda, Lindsey developed friendships with two wives suffering through similar ordeals: Kayla Martinez and Veronica Tejada. Both of their Marine husbands lost both legs to IED blasts. Without needing to say much, each understood what the others were experiencing. They were part of a shared membership in the tiny but growing club of the loved ones of the combat wounded.

In addition to all that she was dealing with as to Trey's health, the wedding plans were a concern. Even though the wedding wasn't until the fall she questioned whether they should postpone the event, downsize it, or even simplify it to a chaplain in the hospital room. Trey had lost his right leg below the knee. He was months away from being fitted for a prosthetic limb. His left leg, though a surgical miracle, was far from healed and amputation was still a possibility. Would he or could he ever walk again, let alone walk down the aisle on his wedding day? Trey's full recovery was her paramount concern, not some ceremony symbolizing their love. She discussed postponing

The wedding. *Myron Hensel Photography*

Left: The vows. *Myron Hensel Photography. Right:* The cake. *Myron Hensel Photography*

the event with her mom, Trey's parents, and the doctors. All were in agreement . . . the wedding needed to proceed, if for no other reason than to give Trey a goal, something to live for, some reason to fight, a reason to walk.

On September 10, 2011—9/10/11—they were married in an outdoor ceremony in Las Vegas. As promised, Trey walked down the aisle. In a comment that still brings tears he told his mom as he began his longest walk, "If I'm going to fall, let me fall." There was a slight limp but for a man who "died twice" and was minutes from losing both legs, it was a remarkable walk.

Lindsey celebrates every step of his recovery and agonizes with every setback. An infection in the nub of his right leg required the removal of two more inches from the stump. Toes on his left foot that continued to curl had to be straightened; the possibility of amputation still lingers. Twenty-two operations later they both hope the surgeries are over and they can move forward. Maybe Trey can't do everything he could before the blast but there are still things he can accomplish. Together they have established new goals. Every morning as they awake in each other's arms, rather than dwelling on what they lost, they focus on what they have.

Natalia and her daddy. *Priscilla Maldonado*

☆ ☆ ☆

A BIRTHDAY WISH

Natalia Maldonado

The twins, Michael and Gabriel, are nine years old. Their dad has been on five combat deployments in their lifetime, earning an assortment of medals and ribbons, including a Bronze Star with a Combat V for valor. The boys know the risks.

Natalia with her twin brothers, Michael and Gabriel. *Priscilla Maldonado*

Mario Maldonado immediately after he was wounded. *Mario Maldonado*

On patrol in Afghanistan. *Mario Maldonado*

Natalia's dad in a Marine armored vehicle in Afghanistan. *Mario Maldonado*

Left: Natalia, Daddy's little girl. *Priscilla Maldonado.*
Right: Natalia missing her daddy on her birthday. *Priscilla Maldonado*

Some of their father's closest friends never made it home and many who did now have artificial limbs. The last time their dad came home from a seven-month Afghanistan deployment, it was early, because an IED nearly destroyed his hand.

It took two surgeries and months of rehabilitation to recover from the wounds that earned Marine Corps Gunnery Sergeant Mario Maldonado a Purple Heart. Now he's gone again. More than most nine-year-olds, they appreciate the costs of freedom.

For their sister, Natalia, who just turned four, it's a little harder to comprehend why he has to be gone so much.

While most four-year-olds look forward to presents, a party, and a birthday cake, all she was hoping for was a phone call. He tried to spoil her on her birthday but it's just not easy half a world away. Natalia, or Booboo, as he calls her, is Daddy's little girl.

He was present for her birth—present, if you count the American Red Cross setting up a phone connection so he could hear her first cries the day she was born. He was in Iraq and wouldn't be home for months.

During that deployment the boys helped care for the newest Maldonado until Dad returned. Their mom, Priscilla, filled a book with pictures of Mario. Michael and Gabriel spent many nights "reading" to their baby sister, showing her the pictures: "This is your daddy. You'll meet

Natalia and her daddy. *Priscilla Maldonado*

The family back together, the day Natalia's daddy was awarded the Bronze Star with Combat V for valor. *Priscilla Maldonado*

him soon." She was "Skypeing" before she could walk or talk, as an unusual father-daughter bond was built prior to them even meeting.

But at four, Natalia knows she isn't old enough, at least not yet. Shortly after her birthday her mom was tucking her in bed and Natalia burst into tears. When Priscilla asked why, Mario's little princess responded, "Because I miss my daddy and love him so much!" Then she added, "I'm just not too much older." Priscilla was confused by what her daughter meant until she clarified, "I'm still too little to go get my daddy so he can come home." Natalia Maldonado may not completely understand but she knows there is a price her family pays so the rest of the nation can live free.

☆ ☆ ☆

PONIES

Lyla's Story

When her older brother, Straton, was two and her daddy was deployed he used to wave at every Marine Corps vehicle that passed and called it his "daddy truck."

Lyla's daddy, standing far left, with his team in Musa Qala, Afghanistan. *Joe Hamer*

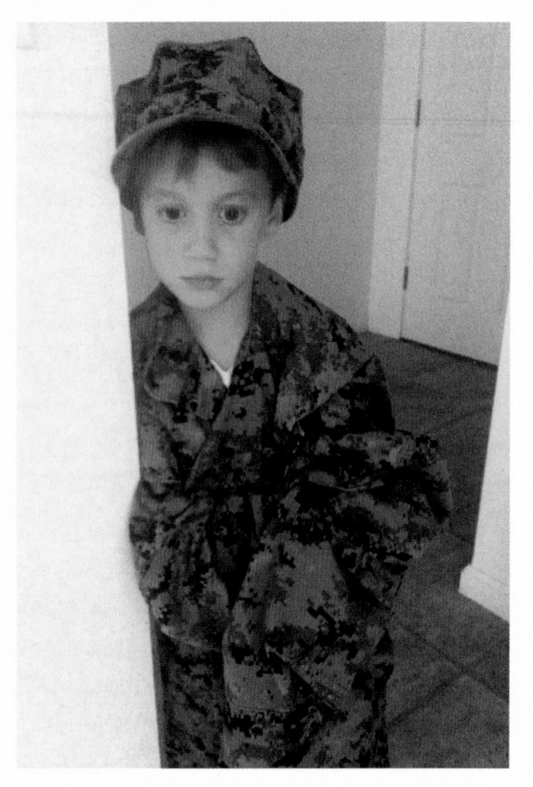

Straton's daddy leaves tomorrow. *Jennifer Hamer*

Once while waiting in the doctor's office he grabbed a book and climbed into the lap of a Marine in uniform, hoping the Marine would read him a story. He missed his daddy, as she does now.

Now her brother is five years old and is the man of the house when their dad is on a "mission." But Lyla doesn't easily submit to anyone's authority. At two, *strong-willed* only begins to describe her; she has a way of commanding attention and getting her way. Yet she is her daddy's little girl and melts his heart.

During the first year of her life, he was out of the country 265 days. He's missed both of her birthdays, being overseas for each celebration. Maybe next year . . .

When her dad is home she likes to climb into his lap and cuddle. He brushes her hair and loves to pull it back into a ponytail. Lyla, though, has

Left: Lyla, a Marine's daughter, strong-willed with a sense of adventure. *Jennifer Hamer*
Right: Lyla and Straton's daddy protecting Afghan children. *Joe Hamer*

Top: A typical Marine gym in Afghanistan. Joe Hamer. *Bottom:* Rush hour on an Afghan highway. Joe Hamer

Lyla without her "ponies." *Bob Hamer*

other plans, often jumping down, ripping out the rubber band, shaking her head until her hair is free, and saying, "No, Daddy, I no like ponies in my hair." Even when her dad tells her how pretty she looks, she refuses to keep the ponytail.

Her dad left on a recent mission and when she waved good-bye she didn't understand he'd be gone for a long time; a two-year-old doesn't quite comprehend the clock or the calendar. She thought he'd be back the next day. When she awoke and her daddy wasn't home her brother had to explain their dad was on another mission. She didn't want to believe it and thought maybe she could coax him home. She grabbed a rubber band, tried to put her hair in a ponytail, and stood at the door. Looking out at the driveway with big tears in her eyes, she shouted, "I like ponies! Please come home, Daddy! I have beautiful ponies in my hair. If you come home I let you put my hair in ponies."

Lyla's daddy with his Afghan "terps." *Joe Hamer*

Top: Lyla and Straton's daddy with an Afghan national policeman in front of a field of opium poppies. *Joe Hamer*
Bottom: Afghan parking lot. *Joe Hamer*

For the next several days, she stood crying at the door, waiting for her daddy, wanting to show him her ponytail . . . but he remained overseas.

Even though he's been gone a long time, as they get into the car Lyla will often pull back her hair and tell her mom, "I go pick up Daddy today and show him my ponies." Someday, maybe soon, when they get in the car they will be picking up her dad and she will finally get her chance. Then they will be together again as a family . . . until the next mission.

When Daddy came home, Lyla and Straton took their parents to see Mickey. *Jennifer Hamer*

4

THREE FLOATING CLOUDS

Leslie Smith

Some people just light up a room. Call it charisma or call it charm, but at social gatherings others gravitate toward them, hoping to share in their magnetism. Typically they tower over the crowd; athletic males, statuesque females, almost larger than life. At five feet one, Army Captain Leslie Smith towers over few but her dazzling smile brightens any venue. People want to share in her confidence and they want to know her story. It isn't until they take a closer look they learn she is missing her left leg. And it isn't until they see "Issac," a yellow Lab and golden retriever mix usually sitting quietly at her feet, and watch the two of them navigate across a room, they realize Leslie is legally blind. Both Leslie and Issac were given twenty-four hours to live and even though this wounded warrior's fight was on a different battlefield, hers is a story worth knowing.

* * *

Born in Winchester, Virginia, she spent most of her youth in Fayetteville, Pennsylvania. The older of two children, Leslie was that girl next door: a high school cheerleader, the homecoming queen, an honor student active in student government. She and her brother Ryan, now an Army

Facing page: In Nashville at the Amputee Fashion Show, sponsored by the Amputee Coalition of America.
Amputee Coalition of America

Leslie's commissioning at Georgetown University. Her father, Nelson Smith, pinning on the gold bars. *Leslie Smith*

In 1999, Leslie deployed to El Salvador with Task Force Hope after Hurricane Mitch. *Leslie Smith*

cardiologist, learned about this nation's core values from patriotic parents. Although her dad spent only six years on active duty in the Army, she loved the stories he shared about his work in the White House Communications Agency during the Kennedy administration. She noted the pride in his voice for having served his country and she sought to serve as well.

At Marymount University in Arlington, Virginia, she majored in communications and was a member of the Army ROTC unit, earning a scholarship after her freshman year. Commissioned a second lieutenant, the lady who avoided math, physics, and chemistry classes in college received orders to the Army's Nuclear, Biological, Chemical (NBC) Corps Officer Basic Course at Fort McClellan, Alabama. Assigned a primary MOS (Military Occupation Specialty) as an NBC officer, she later attended the Defense Information School at Fort Meade, Maryland, picking up a secondary MOS as a public affairs officer (PAO).

As a PAO she found her calling in the military. In 2001 Leslie received orders to Bosnia as part of the NATO-led stabilization mission, Operation Joint Forge.

Working at Eagle Base in Tuzla, Bosnia, her primary responsibility was to plan and accompany distinguished visitors who came to the country to view the work of the multinational peacekeeping forces.

Interacting with politicians and celebrities like Arnold Schwarzenegger, Wayne Newton, Clint Black, and Jessica Simpson was interesting, but her greatest thrill was working daily with the Bosnian people so appreciative of the U.S. government's efforts to rebuild their war-torn nation.

Leslie loved her work and was making plans to extend her tour of duty in Bosnia. The paperwork had been submitted and things were shaping up for a back-to-back deployment. But two weeks before the completion of her first deployment, a complication surfaced impacting the rest of her life.

Her left leg became discolored, began to swell, and was painful to the touch. She initially thought she'd pulled a muscle and could work through the discomfort. As the condition persisted it was getting more difficult to walk; almost dragging the leg as she went about her daily duties. Rest and ice didn't work, and when over-the-counter pain relievers failed, she decided to check in at the base clinic and have the doctors examine her leg. An ultrasound revealed a blood clot, diagnosed as a deep-vein thrombosis. Though she realizes now how serious a blood clot can be, it was difficult at the time to understand the sense of urgency on the part of the medical staff in Bosnia.

The doctors prescribed warfarin and heparin, anticoagulants that act as blood thinners. Warfarin reduces the body's level of vitamin K, essential for clotting. Lower levels of the vitamin

Leslie packed and ready for deployment to Bosnia in 2001. *Leslie Smith*

decrease the body's ability to produce blood clot formations. Heparin is designed to break down existing clots. The side effects of both drugs include abnormal, sometimes profuse internal bleeding. Knowing the need for careful monitoring while on a regimen of both drugs, the brigade surgeon ordered Leslie back to the United States without delay.

Set on remaining in Bosnia for a second deployment, Leslie was now being told to return to the United States even before her initial tour was completed. She was embarrassed by the special treatment she felt she was receiving, wondering how others would view her invisible medical condition and an early trip home. She was also concerned about

Leslie at Eagle Base, Bosnia. *Leslie Smith*

Leslie with "the Terminator" in Bosnia. *Leslie Smith*

long-term effects this might have on her career. She was Army Strong, with career goals, and didn't want this to appear as weakness by her peers and superiors. She had been trained to complete the mission. It was instilled in her in ROTC and every military school she attended. A soldier's mentality is mission first, and it was as if she were putting self above service, a label no one seeks. She at least wanted to stay until her unit rotated home in a few weeks. But it was a losing battle as her pleas to the commanding general and brigade surgeon fell on deaf ears.

She arrived at McGuire Air Force Base at Fort Dix, New Jersey, with little more than the clothes on her back; her personal belongings, gear, and equipment were scheduled to return with her unit. Met by military personnel at the airport, Leslie was promptly processed through the usual paperwork of a soldier returning stateside and immediately transported to Walter Reed Army Medical Center in Washington, D.C.

The doctors tried to diagnose Leslie's condition and identify the cause of the blood clot in her leg. The numerous blood transfusions she received added to the sense of urgency in her treatment. Her parents arrived at the hospital as reality set in. This was no longer an inconvenience interfering with a deployment and career plans: the complications from blood clots were many and potentially fatal. In a week her condition stabilized and she was released from Walter Reed, returning to her parents' home to mend.

Within a few months, new complications arose: blood thinner–induced skin necrosis, a rare side effect of the anticoagulant treatment. Her body was eating itself. Typically the reaction manifests within a week to ten days of taking the drug; this had taken months. As Leslie and the doctors were about to learn, she was anything but typical.

Readmitted to Walter Reed, she was a medical celebrity as doctors who only read about the condition paraded in and out of her room to view the syndrome. The change in the blood thinner treatment allowed her body to stabilize and she was released, preparing for a return to duty and normalcy.

Without warning and with no associated trauma, spontaneous bleeding erupted in her left leg. It began as a pink spot and soon enlarged as the area became inflamed. Once again she returned to Walter Reed and a medical staff puzzled by this young Army captain's condition.

She described the pain "as if razor blades were slicing my legs. It was intense and unbearable." At one point, as she was transferring from the bed to a wheelchair, the pain was so intense she nearly passed out. She felt her eyes roll into the top of her head and before all went black she wondered if she was dying. A massive infusion of pain medication eased the agony, but her life now hung in the balance.

Even with constant monitoring in the ICU, her condition worsened and the medical staff called a Code Blue. It was then she had the first "moment," the one some speak of but often in hushed tones, fearing what others might think. To this day the vision is still clear in her mind. She was separated from her body, looking down from above, watching as a team of doctors treated her. She was gasping for air, staving off death, wanting time to say good-bye to her parents. To the side of the room she saw her dog of years past, Sagi, short for Sagittarius, and her grandmother who died of cancer years earlier. It was as if both were waiting for her on the other side, but she wasn't ready to go. She still had to say her good-byes and she still had a mission to complete. Refusing to surrender, she wouldn't let go, scratching and clawing to survive as the moment passed.

With a tear in her voice, reflecting on her grandmother's death at fifty-six, Leslie says she has often felt her grandmother's presence since that day and wonders whether God didn't take Gram early to be the guardian angel Leslie was going to need as she continued the journey.

Her parents and Ryan were at her side as her three aunts and their husbands from Pennsylvania joined them. Even General Daniel E. Long Jr., the deputy commander in Bosnia, and his wife came to the hospital and stayed with Leslie's family. She was placed in an "imminent death status" and given twenty-four hours to live. She was not expected to survive the night, and her family was instructed to say their final good-byes. Her body was starting to clot itself to death, forming thousands of masses, which doctors predicted would eventually lead to massive tissue damage and complete organ failure. The staff suspected she'd be dead by four the next morning. A social worker was brought in to discuss funeral arrangements and her parents were asked if Leslie was to be buried at Arlington National Cemetery or taken home.

But the doctors at Walter Reed didn't give up. Throughout the night they continued to search for a cure, consulting medical professionals around the world. Her condition was diagnosed as disseminated intravascular coagulation (DIC), which few survive. Doctors were unable to find another case presenting identical symptoms but explained to her parents there might be hope in another medicine, Refludan, an anticoagulant prescribed when heparin is contraindicated. They offered no guarantees, suggesting the medicine might cause immediate death,

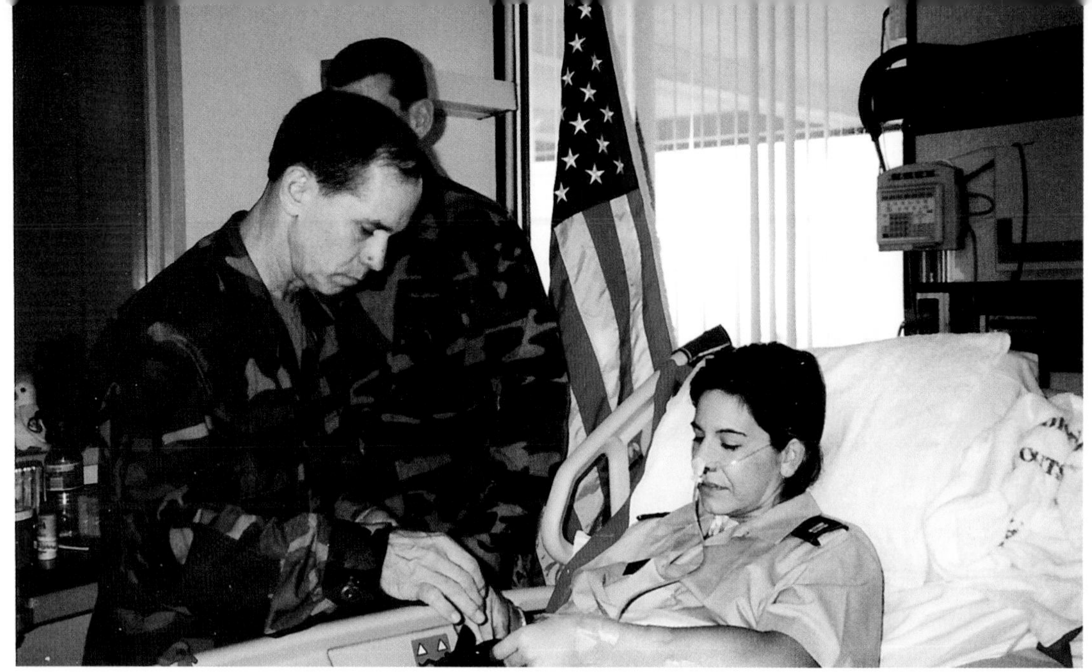

General Daniel E. Long Jr. visiting with Leslie at Walter Reed. *Leslie Smith*

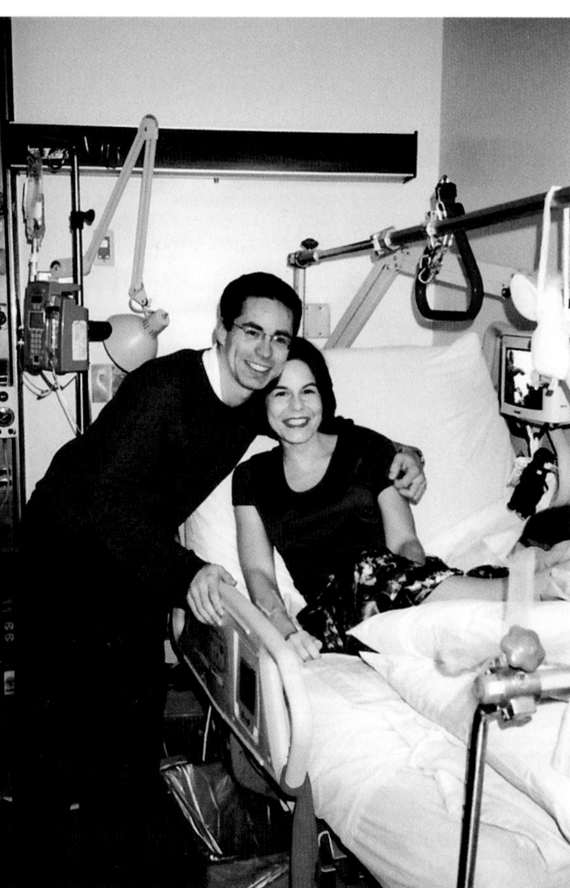

Leslie with her brother, Ryan. *Leslie Smith*

stealing a couple of hours from the doctors seeking to find a better solution. When life hangs in the balance as the body is shutting down, the cause of death doesn't seem that important. Left untreated she was certain to die in a matter of hours, but the suggested treatment offered the potential of instantaneous death by stroke or heart attack. The family decided to take the risk.

Leslie's body responded enough to stay alive, as Refludan slowed the potential systemic collapse. However, she wasn't out of the woods: there was massive tissue damage to her lower body. A team of doctors with their various specialties hovered in the room: hematology; infectious disease; orthopedic. She was still a medical curiosity and the best minds at Walter Reed were determined to save her life. Although she was heavily medicated, she recalls looking at her lower left leg and seeing a deep purple, almost black mass. She begged for a cold Pepsi, but was given only a sip. As she was being wheeled into surgery she remembers one doctor saying, "Don't you die on me."

The doctors were hoping to salvage the leg but there was nothing left to save. Internally the left leg was a jelly-like substance. It had to be amputated and the dying flesh on other parts of her body needed to be removed. Although they couldn't save the leg, they saved her life.

Her mother was by her side and as the anesthesia wore off, Leslie awakened to learn of the amputation. She knew this was life-changing and said, "I used to be a cheerleader." Her mom responded, "Yes, and now you can be the coach."

There was considerable tissue loss to the lower body. During the surgery doctors inserted a vacuum pack, which needed to be surgically changed every three days. In essence the device was sucking out the infection and dead tissue that consumed much of her legs and thighs.

Being a female brought on questions not asked by her injured and wounded male counterparts. With a smile she says, "I loved my shoes and wondered if I would ever wear high heels again." She admits to feeling "very ugly" when she first looked in the mirror, seeing the missing leg and the ravaged flesh on her thighs. She was disfigured and deformed, not the way a woman wants to be viewed. She wanted to lock herself in the house and never face the public again, knowing few would ever understand her plight. Initially there was the shock of the trauma, then the sadness, and finally the anger.

You don't go through a physical and psychological ordeal of amputation without experiencing an emotional roller coaster. Questions abound beyond just the "Why me?" How will I ever live a normal life? How will people view me? Will I be accepted for who I am rather than what I am? There was a small window in which she wallowed in the pity but then one morning in the quietness of her hospital room she found her answer, that second moment, and rather than "Why me?" she asked, "Why not me?" She had a choice. She could play the victim card or accept the

Left: Leslie with the man who was going to give her a new leg, prosthetist Dennis Clark. *Leslie Smith.*
Right: Leslie applying polish to her new toes. *Leslie Smith*

challenge. Sometimes the only route is straight ahead and she took it, refusing to submit or surrender.

As she was rehabbing from the amputation, the first wave of casualties from Iraq and Afghanistan were arriving at Walter Reed. She approached young soldiers in physical therapy who looked as if the future was bleak. She introduced herself and it was obvious the men, many just teenagers, assumed this was one more government official seeking to check off the box "visited the wounded." Then she would pull up her sweatpants leg and reveal the prosthetic limb. An immediate connection was made and Captain Leslie Smith was able to serve in a unique way, offering support, sharing her perspective, helping them find their hidden fortitude.

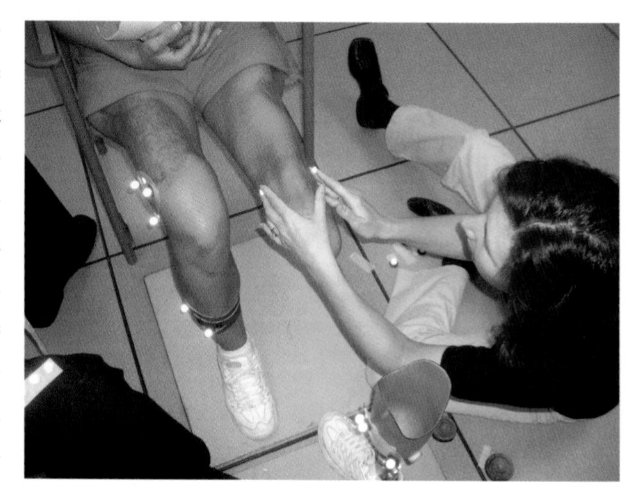

At Walter Reed's Gait Lab applying sensors to calibrate gait and balance. *Leslie Smith*

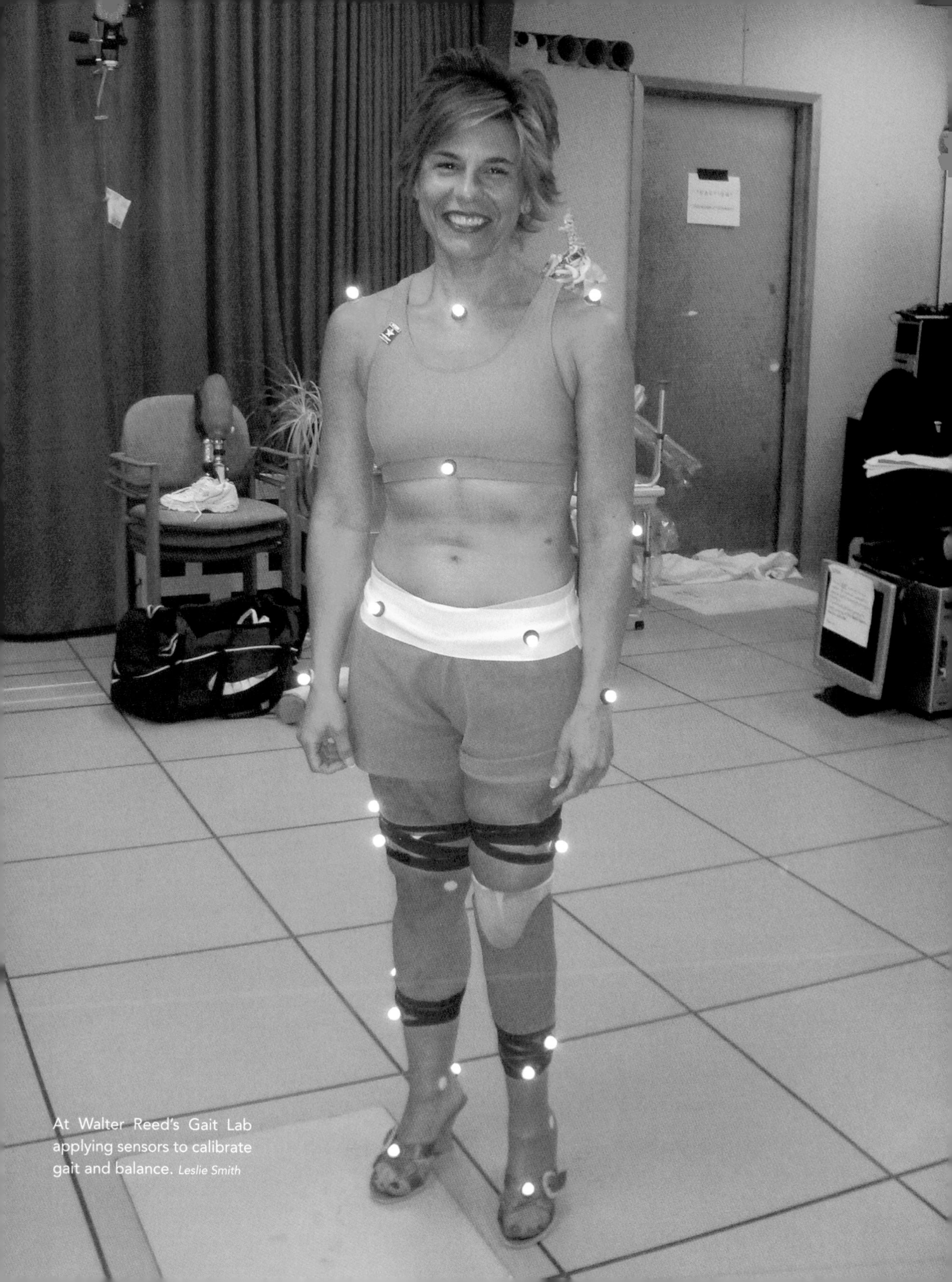

At Walter Reed's Gait Lab applying sensors to calibrate gait and balance. *Leslie Smith*

Leslie and fellow amputees at Walter Reed. *Leslie Smith*

She was able to answer their questions: Do you still have pain? How long before I can walk? Can you run yet? When she first arrived at Walter Reed the doctors couldn't even show her a prosthetic device. Now she was able to show these young soldiers not only the leg but how well it functioned. She led by example. The guilt she first felt for not being injured in combat dissipated as she began to connect with soldiers facing amputation and a lifetime of scars.

* * *

For many of the combat wounded their injuries are complete when the IED explodes or the bullet shatters their bodies. The TBI, traumatic brain injury, may linger or the PTSD, post-traumatic stress disorder, may result in recurring nightmares, but new physical wounds don't surface. For Leslie, the amputation of her left leg was only the beginning.

She spent seven months rehabilitating at Walter Reed. Medically retired from the Army, she began work at USO World Headquarters in Arlington and then as a public affairs specialist at the Joint Warfare Analysis Center. She was on the mend, physically, mentally, and spiritually. A missing leg didn't slow her down as she snow-skied, ran marathons, and competed in a triathlon. She continued to reach out to injured servicemen and -women and even served as a mentor for children with disabilities. She continued to march, refusing to let her injury slow her down. Then tragedy struck a second time.

In 2005, with no symptoms alerting her to the pending loss, she awoke one morning with a severe headache and was rushed to the hospital. Doctors were unable to diagnose the exact cause, suspecting a possible stroke. Whatever the reason, the result was devastating. She lost the vision in her left eye.

The next year the same symptoms reappeared. Her brother, Ryan, now an Army doctor stationed in Hawaii, learned of her condition and immediately called a nearby VA hospital and alerted the doctors to Leslie's medical issues. With only a ninety-minute window in which to work, she was rushed to the VA facility where the physicians were prepared for her arrival. Thanks to Ryan's advance notice, they were able to save the vision in her right eye . . . but it was a short-lived victory.

In 2010 came more heartbreak. Waking with a severe headache, she was again rushed to the hospital. This time the doctors couldn't perform a complete miracle. She lost most of the vision in her remaining eye. The doctors cannot guarantee she won't suffer total blindness in the future.

Originally diagnosed with a rare blood disorder, Factor V Leiden, which put her at a higher risk for blood clots, medical professionals now believe that has very little to do with her condition. Dismissing the initial diagnosis, doctors at Johns Hopkins attribute the problem to a chemical agent or toxin that somehow entered her body, but they have no diagnosis. In medical terms it's called "idiopathic," which means unknown, and she lives with it daily. If she were battling cancer or an identifiable disease she would know what she is fighting, what to expect, but she awakens each morning to the unknown. As one doctor told her, "This is one of the most complex cases I've seen and I deal with the most extreme. I don't know what to tell you."

☆ ☆ ☆

During this journey she found a new companion who was also given twenty-four hours to live. Issac was a day away from being euthanized at a Myrtle Beach, South Carolina, animal shelter. Passing a temperament test and a health screening, he was rescued by the Carolina Canines for Veterans program and trained by Marines serving time at the Camp Lejeune Marine Corps base brig.

Leslie and Issac were partnered in 2009 and have been inseparable ever since. Not only is Issac her eyes when they are out of the house, but he does the laundry, picks up items she drops at home, and brings her what she needs every morning to put on her prosthetic leg. One day while sitting on the side of the bed shortly after losing most of the vision in her right eye, she began to cry and tears tracked her cheeks. Sensing something was wrong, Issac walked over and as her head was bowed, he lifted his and licked away her tears.

General George Patton described success as how high you bounce once you hit bottom. Amputation, the loss of one eye, and the loss of most of the vision in the other eye seem like bottom. But Leslie Smith wasn't about to let her missing leg and blindness define her. She experienced life through the storm and is better for it.

Following the loss of her leg, Leslie saw a psychiatrist who told her there would come a day when she would scream and cry and curse the world. "You will have a total breakdown and it's okay." That day has never come, even as she lives with the unknown. She didn't share this story with the psychiatrist but she shares it now.

A few days after the amputation, it was midmorning and her room was empty, which was unusual. If doctors, nurses, and hospital staff weren't in the room usually her mother was. Her mom was a constant companion providing strength and support. But on this morning Leslie was alone. The TV was off and she was propped up on pillows peering down at her missing leg. In the stillness of the room and without warning a sense of joy—not happiness, but pure joy—overcame her. It came down as if from heaven, entering through her head, as she felt it tingle

Leslie and Issac visit the place where he was trained. *Leslie Smith*

Left: Hiking with Issac. *Leslie Smith. Right:* The Memorial Day celebration on the Mall in Washington, D.C. *Leslie Smith*

slowly through her body, down her arms, and finally out her right foot. She had no comprehension of being in a hospital room as she was transformed beyond Walter Reed. She spied three identical doors resting on three floating clouds. The room was white, the doors were white, the clouds were white. As she focused on the doors, all three opened at the same time. A peace gripped her and never let go, sustaining her throughout the journey.

For years Leslie questioned what those doors represented. At first she assumed they symbolized her successes: her first marathon; her first triathlon; skiing on one leg. But she suspected there was more. On the tenth anniversary of losing her leg she began to understand that day in the quietness of her hospital room. Those doors represented the three challenges she was about to face: first her left leg, then her left eye, then her right eye. Each time she lost a *piece* of her physical body, she found new *peace* as extraordinary opportunities presented themselves. Rather than give up because of the devastation, there is the excitement of "What's next?" Since that day in a quiet hospital room at Walter Reed Army Medical Center, she has spoken at the Republican National Convention, acted in *Days of Our Lives* and *Criminal Minds,* appeared on *Project Runway All-Stars,* been named as "ambassador" for actor Gary Sinise's foundation, representing him

With actor Joe Mantegna on the set of *Criminal Minds*. Bob Hamer

at various venues, and has done public service advertisements for such charities and organizations as the USO, Toyota, Fatigues to Fabulous, the Department of Veterans Affairs' national campaign "Make-the-Connection," the Fisher House Foundation, Freedom Alliance, and Canines for Veterans.

Speaking at the Republican National Convention. *Leslie Smith*

Leslie has been able to share her story with thousands and continues to inspire those she touches. She believes God had to have her prepped as an amputee to help the wounded coming after her and the broken she has yet to meet. Her mission wasn't over when she was sent home early from Bosnia . . . it was just beginning!

☆ ☆ ☆

THE HOLLEY PROVISION

Matthew Holley

It was a matter of hours before Army Specialist Matthew John Holley was scheduled to arrive home.

He was returning early from his deployment to Iraq but not to the welcoming shouts deserving of a hero. He was returning in a flag-draped coffin, killed in action a week earlier. When John and Stacey Holley arrived at the funeral home to make the final arrangements, they learned their twenty-one-year-old son would be offloaded from the cargo hold of a commercial airliner like a commodity pallet shipped in interstate commerce—a forklift hauling the body to a freight terminal, where he would wait with crates of produce and dry goods until the body was claimed.

John and Stacey met in the Army while on active duty and instilled in their only child a love of God and country. They were patriots who raised a warrior willing to serve when far too few answered the call.

Our nation was at war and it was only a matter of time before their son would be fighting half a world away. Like many parents they were proud of their son's decision but fear lingered. Now that fear had become a reality.

Once John learned of the procedure for transferring Matthew's body from the plane to the funeral home, he was on the phone. His son died in service to his country and deserved to be treated like the hero he was. It was a time of great sorrow, massive tears, and broken hearts but not a time to surrender. John would not back down; his son would be honored.

Army Specialist Matthew John Holley. *John Holley*

Top: Even before going into the Army he excelled at the martial arts. *John Holley. Left:* John and Stacey Holley with their warrior son. *John Holley*

Matthew Holley, an American Hero, on duty in Iraq. *John Holley*

Matthew Holley: in the Iraqi desert. *John Holley*

Matthew Holley: in an armored Humvee. *John Holley*

Like so many other American troops, Matthew Holley became the protector of Muslim women and children. *John Holley*

The airlines said no, citing security and procedural concerns, but the persistence of a grieving parent prevailed. Within a matter of hours, miraculously, Matthew Holley did receive a hero's welcome. An honor guard stood at attention at the rear bay of the plane as passengers peered out the windows of the terminal, witnessing the homecoming of a fallen warrior.

Many parents would be satisfied their child received justice but the Holleys wanted more. It was not just their son who merited such respect; it was every fallen serviceman and -woman. Rather than retreat to the shadows of despair, they fought all the way to the halls of Congress to ensure every returning hero is treated with dignity, honor, and the utmost respect. . . . The Holley Provision, signed into law in 2007 as part of the Defense Authorization Act, became Matthew Holley's legacy, the legacy of a hero.

The book John and Stacey Holley wrote about their son. *John Holley*

The day Gabe deployed, smiling through the tears. *Kayla Martinez*

5

THEN HE HEARD THE VOICE

Kayla and Gabe Martinez

Throughout his somewhat brief tenure in the Marine Corps, explosives consumed much of his of work, but this detonation was the loudest he'd ever heard . . . maybe that's because he was part of the blast. Corporal Gabe Martinez saw nothing but brown: the dirt and sand cascading all around as he flew high above the ground. His mouth and nose were filled with the remnants of a primitive highway. Suddenly his life was in slow motion as he hung in the air for what seemed like forever. A certain peace overcame him even though he was in the middle of war-torn Afghanistan.

In an instant he landed and the world was back to full speed, reality settling in: his left leg off to the side; his right foot resting on top of his chest, attached to his body by a few strands of sinew. His first thoughts were of his fellow Marines. Was anyone else hurt? He was a team leader and he had responsibilities. Explosion or no explosion, he needed to act. He needed to complete the mission. Then he heard the Voice.

Prior to deploying, Gabe had told Kayla, "If I lose any of my limbs I want to die." He said the same kind of things to his men as they prepared for missions outside the semi-safe confines of their FOB. Half jokingly he suggested he'd commit suicide if he were seriously injured. Most agreed with Gabe, and displaying the gallows humor of men at war they'd laugh, "Dude, give me a cigarette, then shoot me!" But on this day fantasy became reality. He was catastrophically injured and God gave him a choice. "Gabe, do you want to live?" He heard the Voice as clearly as if his men were speaking to him. He was having a one-on-one with God and without hesitation Gabe responded, "Yes, Lord, I want to live!"

☆ ☆ ☆

For the wives of the wounded, most are eventually asked, "I don't understand. How are you able to handle it?" In describing her journey, Kayla Martinez with her long blond hair, beautiful smile, and perfect complexion says, "It was as if I were running through a dark tunnel not knowing what direction to go, so I just closed my eyes and kept running. Looking back I realize how detached I was from my feelings. Maybe I don't need to grieve much or maybe I just really need to grieve." For this wife of a combat-wounded Marine, the grief was beyond the devastating injuries to her husband.

Her mother was the youngest of twelve and her father the middle of five children. Aunts, uncles, and cousins frequently gathered for weekend events. Friday nights were spent with her mom's side of the family and Sundays were reserved for her dad's relatives. Her "dark tunnel" journey began in October 2009, when Kayla's dad shocked those at a family outing by announcing, without much fanfare, the doctors discovered a tumor in his colon and he was scheduled for surgery in two weeks.

Gabe and Kayla Martinez at the Marine Corps Birthday Ball. *Kayla Martinez*

The shock of her dad's announcement was still fresh in her mind when a week later the grandfather who taught her to dance and taught her to laugh took an uncharacteristic fall at Kayla's house. Refusing any help, he remained on the floor looking toward the sky through the glass ceiling of the sunroom he and Kayla's father built years earlier. It was almost as if he were seeking answers while contemplating life. Later that evening, after returning home, her grandfather said he was going to lie down in his office in the back of the house. There was no stress in his voice, no submission, just weariness. A short time later a shot rang out. When Kayla's grandmother rushed to the back of the house, she found her husband of sixty-five years slumped in his chair, a gun by his side.

Kayla's pain was far from over. The day after her grandfather's funeral, her dad had nineteen polyps removed from his colon. Although the doctors didn't believe the polyps to be cancerous, they wanted him to start a mild-dosage chemotherapy pill once he healed. The recovery process, however, was more difficult than the doctors predicted. Plagued by infections and more surgeries to clean out the infections, he didn't begin the chemo therapy until six months after the first surgery. A follow-up examination months later revealed the cancer, which the medical professionals didn't believe he had, metastasized to his lungs.

Gabe and Kayla at their wedding.

Randall Olsen Photography

☆ ☆ ☆

The two met in high school and began dating shortly after graduation in 2007. Gabe had spent three years on active duty in the Marine Corps with one deployment under his belt and now Kayla was about to assume the role of Marine wife.

Surrounded by family and friends, they married on July 30, 2010, as the clouds of despair were pushed away, at least for the day. Her father was healthy enough to walk her down the aisle and dance the father-daughter dance. In less than a year, at fifty-nine years old, he would be gone, cancer ravaging his body, but she will be forever grateful to have shared this special day with him.

With no time for a real honeymoon, Gabe reported to Twentynine Palms, the Marine Corps base in California's Mojave Desert, for one month of training closely followed by the seven-month deployment to Afghanistan.

Still grieving the loss of her grandfather less than a year earlier and the failing health of her father, August brought more stress. Daily the news reported increased casualties in the ever-dangerous Helmand province. Reality set in when the *Marine Corps Times* reported Sergeant Joe Bovia, Gabe's close friend, had been killed in action.

By late September, the anxiety was building. Sleep was not coming easily as she grappled with her father's health and her husband's imminent departure. There were nights she would awake in tears not even remembering her dreams, just knowing incessant fear consumed her. She lost her grandfather, her father was dying, and her husband of less than two months was headed for combat. The three men she loved were breaking her heart; abandoning her in one way or

Marine pre-deployment at Twentynine Palms, California. *DOD*

another. She couldn't imagine living without Gabe. She struggled nightly with dark thoughts as serenity eluded her. One night, however, she was startled from a restless sleep, awaking with a strange peace about the upcoming deployment. It was as if a blanket of tranquility had been laid at the foot of their bed. The poisoned thoughts that permeated her mind evaporated like a mist in the wind . . . she knew her husband was coming home alive! Kayla knew God had plans for them.

A few days before Gabe's October deployment, Gabe introduced his new bride to fellow Marine, Lance Corporal Justin Gaertner. Gabe and Justin were in the same unit, 1st Combat Engineer Battalion/Mobility Assault Company, and were best friends. At dinner Gabe asked Justin if he was taking "civvies" (civilian clothes) to Afghanistan. Without skipping a beat, Justin, who was heading out on his second combat deployment to Afghanistan, replied, "Yeah, man. You have to take at least one pair so when we both get blown up we can walk around Germany together." Little did he know his humor foretold the future.

Combat patrol, Marjah, Afghanistan. *USMC LCpl. Tommy Bellegarde*

☆ ☆ ☆

FEEDBACK

Marla's e-Letter

At nearly every book-signing for these American Heroes works, there will be at least one person in line carrying a picture of a son, daughter, or spouse standing next to me in one of the many battlefields of this long war. Most of the photographs show us clad in flak jackets, helmets, and sweat-soaked, dirty desert camouflage clothing.

The photograph is usually presented with a just-purchased book and a request for me to sign both. For most authors this would likely be a pleasant occasion—a fan buying a book for another fan! But for me these are moments fraught with great anxiety, for I rarely know if the person standing beside me in the photo is still alive. Too often bearers of these pictures have presented them to me with a statement like "Please sign this photo of my son and you in Afghanistan. A few weeks after it was taken he was killed by a roadside bomb. . . ."

Signing books at a military exchange. *Premiere*

Words like these are heartbreaking. I can feel the grief and anguish of the Gold Star spouse, parent, or child of the slain warrior and see the pain in their eyes. Invariably I lose it—and the entire line of book buyers comes to a halt in the midst of shared sadness.

Given experiences like this, imagine the joy of receiving feedback like that contained in the email below. It was sent to me after a book signing at the Camp Pendleton Marine Corps Exchange (MCX) in mid-February 2013.

Dear LtCol North:

Thank you for taking a moment to speak with me last week at Camp Pendleton MCX. You were very kind to a proud mom, shoving a photo under your nose!

The picture of my son and you was taken in Ramadi 2004. At the time I believe you were attached to his unit; 2nd Bn, 4th Marines he was a Sgt. He was wounded not too long after, in August of that year. He recovered and has continued his career in the Marines. After completing a stint at recruiting, he was accepted into the officer program, graduating from the University of Idaho with honors. He is currently a 1st Lieutenant, stationed at Camp Pendleton with Bravo Co, 1st Law Enforcement Battalion. As I mentioned to you at our meeting, he is scheduled for duty in Afghanistan late April or early May. He will be leading a personal security detail for ███████

On a side note, you also met my father under similar circumstances. You did a speaking engagement at a church in Gresham, Oregon, a few years ago. My dad had a copy of same photo, which you were kind enough to autograph. My son proudly hangs the original in his home.

Thank you again.

A very proud Marine Mom,
Marla

FOB Dwyer, in the middle of nowhere, Helmand Province, Afghanistan. *USMC Lt. Col. Stewart Upton*

On October 9, 2010, Gabe deployed as part of Operation Enduring Freedom. The three-plus-day journey halfway around the world was uneventful, until they made a combat landing into Forward Operating Base Dwyer, in Afghanistan. As if dropping from the sky, the plane dipped quickly from a high altitude, throwing in a few bobs and weaves to avoid a potential ground attack by terrorists. From Dwyer the men convoyed to their new home for the duration of the deployment, Marjah, an unincorporated agricultural district in Helmand Province.

Army General Stanley McChrystal, then commander of all troops in Afghanistan, called Marjah "a bleeding ulcer." In July 2010, the late American diplomat Richard Holbrooke described it as "one of the bellies of the insurgency." It had long been a bastion of Taliban support and Gabe Martinez and his fellow Marines would be operating in one of the most dangerous venues in the world.

The Marines at Marjah were billeted at an outpost large enough to stage vehicles but providing little else in the way of comfort. Living in tents, electricity was produced by fickle generators, drinking water came in plastic bottles, and what little water they had for bathing was trucked in. For the most part, baby wipes replaced showers and the meals were out-of-the-box MREs.

Performing one of the most important missions in the war, the men of Gabe's unit often left in the early morning hours in their overgrown armored mine-detection vehicles called Huskies to begin the daily task of clearing the third-world roadways of Marjah.

The typical route clearance convoy consisted of six vehicles. While men manned the vehicles, dismounted patrols accompanied the convoy. "Intermediate teams" consisting of three to five men were off to the side of the vehicles, usually within twenty-five meters, sweeping for ex-

Top: Sweeping for mines near Marjah, Afghanistan. *USMC Sgt. E. J. Barnes.* *Bottom:* The man with the minesweeper is always all alone out in front. *USMC Cpl. Alfred V. Lopez*

plosives. A second team, also consisting of three to five men, referred to as "hunter-kill teams," flanked fifty to seventy meters ahead of the convoy, looking for insurgents who could remotely detonate explosives.

In an armored convoy Gabe and his combat engineers were the ones who jumped out first to search for IEDs. *Gabriel Martinez*

As technical and complex as the U.S. war machine was, the insurgents were equally adept at causing chaos with comparatively meager resources. Pressure-plate IEDs and loop-switch explosives were common. Utilizing two pieces of metal resembling a makeshift clothespin and whatever explosive devices they could cobble together, the contrivances were effective. When weight was placed upon the object the two metal pieces served as a conductor, detonating the land mine. Loop switches were also primitive but effective. Two bare pieces of wire tied in a loose loop fashion became deadly when a person or object tugged on the wire, thus connecting the stripped ends and completing the circuit, causing the explosion. Most of the IEDs encountered were tripped by Marines on patrol but some were remotely detonated by watchers in the field, hidden some distance from the patrol or convoy, detonating the device when the Marines were in the kill zone. Gabe and his men were responsible for detecting these enemies and their devices.

* * *

When Kayla returned to Colorado after Gabe deployed, normalcy prevailed. She kept busy, completing the final year of her bachelor of fine arts degree, interning at High Noon Entertainment, and helping in her father's window sales company. She once overheard his instructions to an employee to take some tools because he was "dying" and didn't want to burden his wife with disposing of the business. Overhearing such comments allowed Kayla to appreciate the moments they had before he passed.

Communication with Gabe was limited. Clearing routes for military convoys, he would often leave the forward operating base for days at a time, sometimes as long as two weeks. During these missions they would have no contact. When he returned to base for a day or two before his next assignment he could call or Skype.

On Thanksgiving, November 25, Kayla went to Gabe's brother's house for a lunchtime holiday celebration and videotaped the gathering as family members wished the Marine well.

After lunch, she headed to her parents' home, where the extended family offered their best to Gabe on the video Kayla was preparing. As the evening waned, Kayla headed to her cousin Angie's house. Gabe was hoping they could Skype before he left on his next mission but Kayla was unable to get Internet access. Limited now to a phone call, Gabe was mildly irritated when they finally connected, complaining they could only hear and not see each other. In jest, blaming her for not getting Internet access, he said, "You are going to feel bad tomorrow when I get blown up and you never see me again." Kayla gave it right back, telling her Marine to "get over it" and they could Skype tomorrow when he returned from the mission.

* * *

The day started out like any other in Marjah; warm and sunny, the beginning of another hot day. The days in this remote part of the world were hot but the nights frigid. Gabe would often awaken with feet like ice cubes and joked he could stay warm if he didn't have feet. . . . His wish was about to come true!

There was nothing unusual about the morning and Gabe assumed it was going to be like most missions. In the month and a half he'd been "in-country" most patrols found him at one point wading through chest-high canal water and traipsing through acres of marijuana plants taller than a man. Most patrols were uneventful but some resulted in contact with the enemy or the discovery of explosives and weapons caches. On more than one occasion while working the hunter-kill teams a football field away from the convoy, Gabe's metal detector popped positive and buried in a shallow pit were grenades, ammunition, and IEDs.

It was still Thanksgiving night for Kayla and Gabe's unit had been on patrol a little more than an hour. Time seemed to drag but there was no use checking a watch. Marines in Marjah didn't punch a time clock. They worked until the mission was complete. The lead vehicle was slowly moving along a dirt path the team had swept on previous missions. With the simplicity it took to bury an IED, the fact a road had been cleared days earlier was no guarantee it was still safe to travel.

For some unknown reason, the lead Husky's electronic jamming system shut down.

With the electronics on the vehicle "down" it was impossible for the Marines to prevent an IED from detonating. The lead driver stopped the Husky and announced over the radio the equipment was malfunctioning. He was instructed to shut down the system, restart, and proceed.

abe and his men preparing for a patrol. *Gabriel Martinez*

He did as instructed and began slowly moving forward, hoping the restart had worked. It didn't. As the second vehicle followed in trace an explosion ripped through the front end of the armored Husky, shaking the convoy. Controlled chaos prevailed!

Gabe and his best friend, Justin Gaertner, riding in the third vehicle, jumped out, conducting a dismounted protocol sweep of the area. Both Marines focused not just on the immediate ground but scanned the horizon for an insurgent who might have detonated the device. Anytime an IED detonates it can be the signal for an ambush or further explosions. The men were on high alert, performing the delicate mission but ever watchful for insurgents ready to engage in a firefight. Gabe swept the right side of the crippled vehicle and Justin took the left. They were looking for secondary or even tertiary devices planted near the initial site designed to grab any Marine escaping the scene or running to the aid of a downed serviceman.

Part of their responsibility was to also collect the scrap metal from the explosion to prevent the insurgency from using it in some other capacity, such as shrapnel for IEDs or suicide vests. Once Gabe and Justin swept the area, they were to recover the damaged front end of the vehicle and continue the mission. A second IED put those plans on hold.

Without warning Gabe, just a few feet from the damaged Husky, stepped on a hidden pressure-plate device and was propelled high into the air, another victim of the insurgents' wrath. Within seconds he had his conversation with God, choosing to live.

With the determination of a man now on a dual mission to not only survive but also complete his task, he took control. He assessed the situation and prepared to climb out of the huge crater created by the explosion. He assumed he had a concussion and when he foolishly threw his damaged right foot off his chest he realized there was little connecting the leg to the rest of his body. Blood was pouring out of his lower limbs. As he attempted to pull himself out of the hole a third explosion thundered, adding more confusion to the situation, throwing him back into the newly generated depression.

Sergeant Ibrahim Attya and Corporal Spencer Karam jumped into the crevice, administering

Top: Foot patrols through Afghanistan's marijuana fields are a daily occurrence. *Bryan Carter*
Bottom: Whenever possible, Husky mine-detection vehicles lead every convoy. *USMC Sgt. E. J. Barnes*

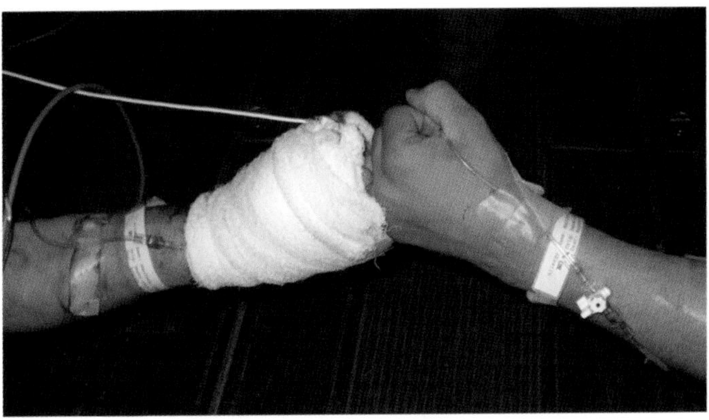

Left: Lance Corporal Anthony Roldan snapped this shot as Gabe and Justin Gaertner were evacuated on a Black Hawk medevac helicopter. *USMC LCpl. Anthony Roldan.* *Right:* Gabe and Justin on the helo. Semper Fidelis! *Gabriel Martinez*

lifesaving first aid, with Corpsman Jared Harper applying tourniquets to stem the bleeding. Gabe remained calm and awake as pain seared his body.

Within minutes a medevac helicopter arrived and as Gabe was being placed on the Army Black Hawk he learned Justin had been seriously wounded in the third explosion.

Justin and Gabe, two Marines, two friends, were on the same chopper, lying side by side, comforting each other, sharing the same turbulent ride. Gabe later said, "I was right there with him and he was right there with me. I was able to reach out and touch his bandaged hand. It was a great pain reliever."

Throughout the ordeal Gabe remained conscious, aware of his surroundings but unaware of the full extent of his injuries . . . both legs destroyed and a fractured skull.

As traumatic as the explosion was, he says the most frightening moment occurred at the Dwyer Combat Support Hospital, or "CASH," as it's called in the military.

While in the middle of surgery, Gabe's eyes burst open, shocked awake from a medically induced sleep. He could see the doctors and hear their voices but was unable to move; strapped to the operating table and paralyzed by the anesthesia. He tried to scream but nothing came from his mouth. Desperately seeking a breath, none came. Spent with fear, he believed death was imminent. He had already told God he wanted to live and questioned why he was dying. No one responded to his silenced pleas. He refused to relax into death; he was going to fight to live.

Within seconds darkness overcame him again and he was no longer in the moment. No one could explain the experience, but Gabe now says with a smile he doesn't expect any medical personnel to enlighten him. Despite missing both legs, no one in authority has ever officially in-

Lifesavers at work in the Triage Ward, U.S. Army Combat Support Hospital, FOB Dwyer, Helmand Province, Afghanistan. *Chuck Holton, FOX News*

formed him his legs were traumatically amputated. He guesses some things, like missing legs and surgical visions, just go unsaid.

* * *

Around nine the next morning, Kayla's cell phone rang. The caller ID displayed an unusual series of numbers. Thinking it was a solicitor, she ignored the call. Every time Gabe called it was a five-digit number, so she didn't believe it was her husband. But as she reflected on the number it seemed familiar, reminding her of a number he used on a previous deployment when he used a satellite phone. Could it have been Gabe? They developed a system where he would call twice in succession, signaling it was him, allowing her to avoid the annoying solicitations.

When the phone rang a second time, the same number appeared on the caller ID. Her birthday was two days away and she thought it strange Gabe would call early, not waiting until her birthday. Kayla tentatively picked up the phone.

"Hello."

"Is this Mrs. Martinez?" a man inquired on the other end.

"Yes."

"Ma'am, one moment, please." Kayla thought of hanging up, thinking it was a solicitor, but for some reason she remained on the line, intrigued by the strange number and her prearranged signal with Gabe.

"Hello," said Gabe in a dry, scratchy voice.

Kayla could tell there was something different in his demeanor but responded, "Hey, what's up?"

"I've been hit," he said.

"What do you mean, you've 'been hit'?"

"I was hit by an IED. . . . I lost both of my legs."

There was no desperation in the warrior's voice. No hint he'd just run the gauntlet of death. He reported the injuries as if he had dented the fender of the family car backing out of the garage.

Kayla paused for a moment, gathering her thoughts, seeking to stem the tide of emotions wanting to erupt. It was no time to panic. She remained stoic as more bad news flooded her mind . . . her grandfather's death, her dad's illness, and now a catastrophically combat-wounded husband.

"Where are you?" she asked.

"I can't tell you," he said, still wanting to maintain operational security.

"No, I mean are you in a hospital?"

"Yeah."

"Are you in Afghanistan?"

"Yeah."

"Where are they taking you next?"

"What?"

"Where are they—"

"Hold on," interrupted Gabe. Then she heard him ask, "Doc, how do you turn the sound up? I can't hear anything." Coming back to Kayla, Gabe said, "Sorry, I can't really hear you and they said this is as loud as they can make it."

"It's okay. Where are they taking you?"

"I'm coming home."

"When?"

"What?"

"When?" now shouting into the phone.

"Sorry, I'm really tired."

"It's okay, how do you feel?"

"Fine."

"How much of your legs did you lose?"

"No one's told me yet. I can't tell but I think one is above the knee and one is below."

"Is the rest of you okay?"

"I lost my legs."

"I know but is there anything else that is hurt?"

"No, I don't think so."

"Well, Gabriel, I am glad you are alive. It's so good to hear you."

There was silence on the other end of the phone.

"Hello? Gabe?"

"Yeah," answered Gabe weakly.

"I love you."

"I love you, too. I have to go. I can't stay awake," said Gabe as the medication was taking its toll.

"Are you going to call your mom or do you want me to talk to her?"

"You call her," he said just above a whisper.

"Okay, call me when you can. I love you."

After Kayla ended the call, the conversation played over and over in her mind as if on a loop, as she processed everything Gabe had said. She needed to notify the family; no time to grieve, no time to mourn. She immediately tried calling Gabe's mom but Kay's phone was dead.

Kayla then called Gabe's younger sister.

"Joy, it's Kayla. Are you with your mom?" Kayla hoped she wasn't betrayed by the near panic in her voice.

"No," said his sister.

"Okay, well, when you talk to her can you have her call me?"

"Sure."

Kayla sensed Joy heard the alarm in her voice as the truth hit her; she was the only one who knew Gabe had been injured. She wanted to be sensitive to the order in which she relayed the news, but she needed to talk to someone just for own well-being. She needed a shoulder. She needed that listening ear to walk her through another nightmare. A thousand miles from Gabe's home base, there were no military families in her life. She knew few of the other wives from Gabe's unit. Her neighbors in Colorado weren't facing deployment, death, and devastating wounds.

Kayla sought order in the fast-developing turbulence. Where should she go first? Since Gabe's mother wasn't home, should she go see her own mom? The trivial seemed comforting as she questioned, "What should I wear?" Then, remembering the urgency of her mission, she realized, "Why does it matter what I wear? Just find something and go!"

In the bathroom she looked in the mirror and saw the tears welling up. She let them stream down her soft cheeks and allowed the tide of emotions to roll. But it was as if the tears brought relief, triggering memories of the dream before Gabe deployed. A new reality emerged: "Why am I crying? He's alive. I got to hear his voice. Get over it and keep moving."

She debated driving to Gabe's mom's house, thirty minutes away, but feared Kay might not be home. It was Black Friday, the day after Thanksgiving, and she assumed her mother-in-law was shopping. Kayla didn't have the luxury of driving all over town hoping to find a relative and didn't want his mother to hear the news from anyone but her. Kayla hopped into the car and headed toward her parents' home.

As soon as she entered the kitchen, where her mother was standing, the despair was evident. "Hey, honey, what's wrong?"

Kayla fought hard to control the emotions beginning to erupt. "Deep breath. Deep breath. Don't cry," she said to herself.

"Kayla, whatever it is you can tell me. It's okay, sweetie."

She held up a slightly quivering hand. "Mom, hold on. I'm going to tell you. I just need a second."

"Okay."

"Gabe got hit by an IED and lost his legs."

"*No!* Are you serious, Kayla?"

"Yes!"

"No! How do you know?"

"Mom, he called me and told me."

Kayla's mom threw her arms around her daughter, each comforting the other. The emotions erupted and the tears flowed.

As Kayla was explaining her efforts to contact Gabe's mom, her phone rang.

"It's Kay. Do I answer it?"

"You have to answer it. She knows something's wrong."

"Do I tell her what happened or do I tell her we are on our way over there and will talk to her when we get there?"

"I don't know, Kayla. Just tell her. She has to know."

"Hello?" answered Kayla.

"Hi there, sorry my phone was dead," said Kay apologetically.

"It's okay. I talked to Gabe this morning," Kayla said, trying to remain calm.

"Okay."

"He got hit by an IED." Kayla knew Gabe's mom had no idea what an IED was or what kind of damage it could do. She thought about leaving it at that and waiting until they were face-to-face to deliver the details but she continued: "He lost both of his legs."

The screams coming out of the phone were horrifying as Kayla's mom took the phone.

Trying to offer a mother's comfort, Judy said, "Kay, I'm so sorry. We are coming over there right now. We are getting in the car. Don't leave. We are coming."

By the time they arrived at the house, a few neighbors had gathered, more flooding in. Kay was crying, blaming herself for not praying enough for her son, asking why God would do this.

Kayla was bombarded by questions for which she had few answers. What's going to happen? What do we need to do? Where is he? When is he coming home? When Kayla tried to reach the unit's family readiness officer, she was out shopping on Black Friday. Her voice mail provided the number for the battalion duty officer. Kayla called the number and spoke with a staff sergeant.

"Hello, Staff Sergeant, my husband called me about an hour ago and told me he was injured in Afghanistan."

"Ma'am, do you know what injuries he sustained?"

"He told me he lost both of his legs but he seemed pretty drugged up, so I really don't know for sure."

"You said he called you?"

"Yes."

"Ma'am, if he sustained those injuries he should still be in surgery and not calling you."

"Well, he did call me and that is what he told me."

"So, what are you trying to figure out?"

"Anything!" said Kayla, exasperated she had to spell out her concerns. "All I know is what he told me. I don't know where he is. I don't even know what happened. I want any information I can get."

The conversation continued as the Marine staff sergeant tried to look up Gabe in the system. Unable to find any information, he told Kayla there was no Gabriel Martinez at the unit. Kayla explained Gabe was attached to a tank platoon out of Twentynine Palms, not 1st Combat Engineers, his unit at Camp Pendleton. The frustration built as the staff sergeant argued the Marine Corps wasn't deploying tanks to Afghanistan.

When Kayla provided the address where Gabe was receiving mail, he told her the address didn't exist. Irritation turned to anger when Kayla said, "For an address that doesn't exist, my husband somehow manages to receive the packages I send him." But all this was irrelevant. She wasn't interested in debating combat troop deployment. She knew her husband was injured and she sought answers. The staff sergeant said he would see what he could do and call back.

Thirty minutes later, there was a loud knock at the door. By now at least twenty people were in Kay's home, all standing in a circle praying for Gabe. When Gabe's youngest brother, Clint, answered the door Kayla spied two Marines in uniform. Kayla knew the protocol. If a Marine is injured the family receives a phone call. If a Marine dies, a notification team pays a personal visit. Fear engulfed her as her body began to shake, overcome by panic. She feared the worst, believing Gabe was dead!

When the Marines stepped inside the door they were overwhelmed and confused by the number of people in the house. Their mission was to deliver a casualty report to the family and had no idea Gabe had already called reporting his injuries to his wife.

Dressed in a khaki uniform top with ribbons spread across his left pocket and blue trousers with the blood stripe down the seam, the Marine began to read the casualty report explaining the circumstances surrounding the injury. The female Marine stood to the side, quiet, not smiling, adding to the solemnity of the moment. As if in slow motion, the words trickled from the Marine's mouth. Kayla began to go to those dark places no spouse ever wants to visit. Visions of her husband's death besieged her. She would never hear Gabe's voice or hold him or make love with him. She was only half listening, the words slowly echoing in the canyons of her mind until she heard, "Gabriel is alive."

What! She wanted to strangle the Marine! Why in the world couldn't he have started the conversation with those words?

Kayla understood it was a difficult assignment to notify family members their loved one was injured or dead, but she would have liked more answers. It was obvious the Marines were short on details. The family drilled them on where Gabe was going, what clothes and supplies he needed, where he would be taken and treated. Once the Marines left and with many questions unanswered, Kayla called her favorite staff sergeant.

"Hi. I just wanted to call back and let you know the Marines came to my door."

"Oh, good, I figured they would." Kayla kept her cool but wanted to shout, "You figured? Why would you not tell me that in the first place?"

* * *

The hours crept by as Kayla waited for news as to when she could see her husband. She knew others meant well but many were offering advice, pressuring her to make decisions she was unprepared to make. Veterans of previous wars with experience dealing with the VA insisted Kayla needed to begin applying for various programs and finding medical care. They pressed for immediacy and Kayla was still grieving, trying to process what happened and what the future held. Fortunately, her Marine Corps liaison provided the help she needed and lessened the burden others were placing upon her.

The word finally came. Gabe was being transferred from Landstuhl, Germany, to the Naval Medical Center in Bethesda, Maryland. The military agreed to fly Kayla and Gabe's mom there. The nonprofit organization Fisher House, which provides housing for the loved ones of military personnel being treated for their wounds, also administers Hero Miles. The program furnished airline tickets for Gabe's four brothers and sisters.

They arrived at Bethesda around ten o'clock at night and were greeted just inside the door by the sculpture *The Unspoken Bond,* a Navy corpsman holding a wounded Marine in his arms. Kayla knew that bond had saved her husband's life.

Running down the hallway, all were anxious to see Gabe. Clint was leading the way but Kay told him he needed to wait, saying Kayla had to be the first family member into the room. When they arrived at the room, the staff sergeant who accompanied them at the hospital entered first.

"Corporal Martinez."

"Yes, Staff Sergeant."

"I have a surprise for you."

Kayla raced to the bed and hugged her husband as tight as she could for an extended moment, then stepped away so the rest of the family could say hello. Both of Gabe's eardrums were ruptured, so it was difficult for him to hear, smiles and hugs doing most of the talking. Kayla was suffering from a severe head cold and the cross-country flight did nothing to alleviate the congestion, so it was difficult for her to hear as well. They were the perfect couple . . . yelling how much they loved each other.

Shrapnel wounds were visible on his face, hands, and what was left of his legs. A large U-shaped gash on his forehead was the result of metal that penetrated his Kevlar helmet, fracturing his skull and causing bleeding on the brain. When Gabe's mom said she hoped the scar on his forehead would heal, Gabe quickly replied, "I don't."

"Why would you want this big ugly scar on your forehead?" she asked, confused by his quick response.

"I think it's pretty cool. I hope it looks like a sweet battle scar the rest of my life." Apparently two missing legs weren't sufficient battle scars for the combat-tested Marine.

Kayla showed him the video clips she recorded on Thanksgiving. She could tell it was hard

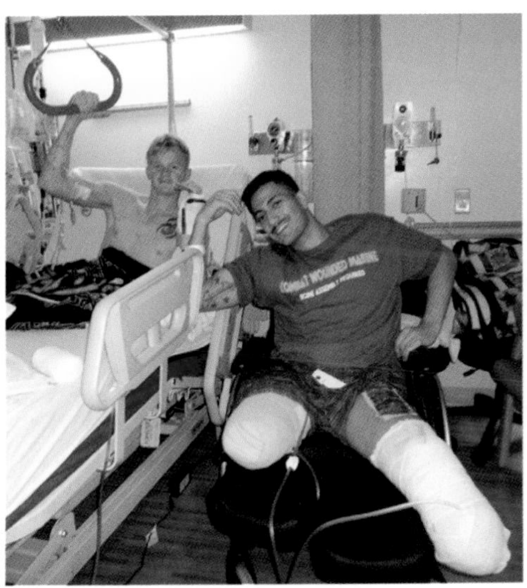

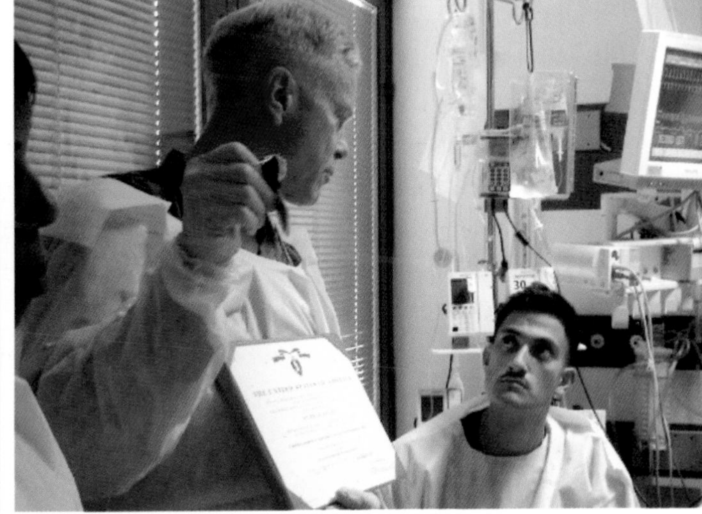

Left: Justin and Gabe at Bethesda. *Kayla Martinez. Right:* General James F. Amos, commandant of the Marine Corps, presents Gabe with the Purple Heart. *Kayla Martinez*

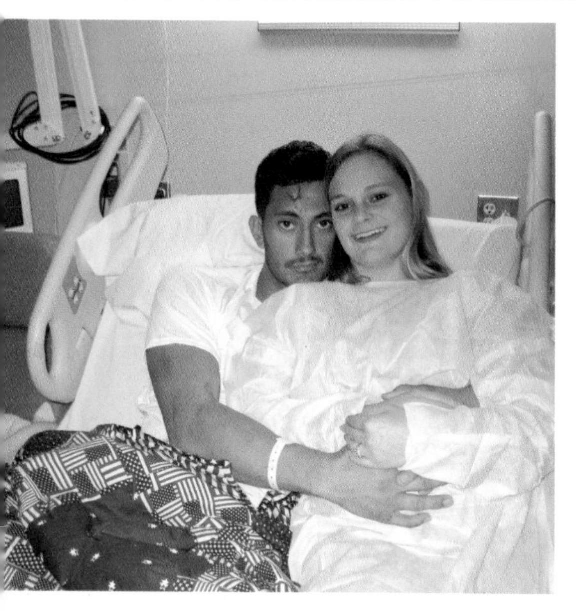

Gabe and Kayla at Bethesda. *Kayla Martinez*

for Gabe, a modest warrior, to watch as everyone said they were so proud of him, thankful for everything he was doing, and hoping he would return home safely. As difficult as it was to watch, it was good for him to see everyone from back home and know they had been cheering him on and praying for him.

Kayla and the family stayed at the Navy Lodge on the hospital grounds. The next morning she was eager to get back to Gabe and was up and out the door early. Since it was faster to walk than wait for the shuttle, she and Angelina, Gabe's sister, enjoyed the walk. When they got up to Gabe's room his brother Angelo was already there with oatmeal and hot chocolate from McDonald's. Having not eaten much since the blast, Gabe recalls it was the best oatmeal and hot chocolate he'd ever tasted.

He was in great spirits and seemed to be adjusting well once he overcame a major obstacle: he forgot how to move what remained of his legs. For some reason the brain told the body the legs were missing and refused to command what was left to move. He could outshine any patient at the pull-up bar but could not wiggle his damaged limbs. During one session with the physical therapist, she was manually moving his legs, one traumatically amputated above the knee and one below. As the medical professional manipulated the limbs, she kept inquiring if Gabe could do it on his own, without her help. He wanted to but for some reason the brain wouldn't engage. As she continued the exercise, she pulled her hands away unbeknownst to Gabe and he continued to move his legs without her assistance. What to many would seem like a minor accomplishment was in fact a major miracle. Gabe was ready to tackle rehabilitation with an inner strength allowing him to surmount whatever obstacle lurked beyond the next medical procedure.

Improvement came quickly. In less than a month he was ready to move to the Naval Medical Center in San Diego, near his unit at Camp Pendleton.

Gabe made a remarkable recovery and quickly began the process for being fitted with prosthetic legs.

Within months he was walking. By Easter, 2011, he and Kayla returned to Denver for a hero's welcome. The joy of seeing family and friends for the first time since the injuries of Thanksgiving was offset by Kayla's dad's failing health. The cancer had metastasized to his brain.

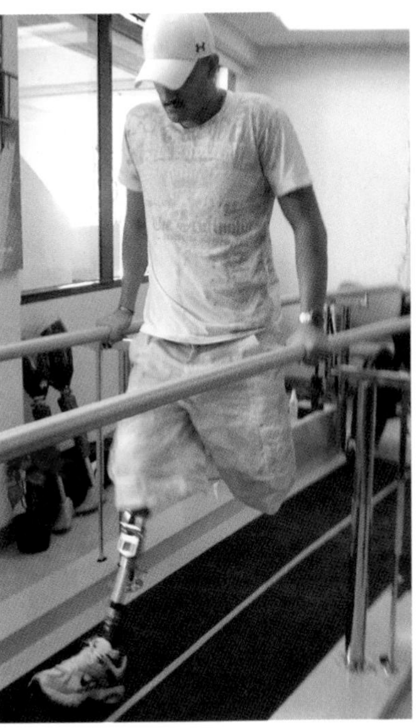

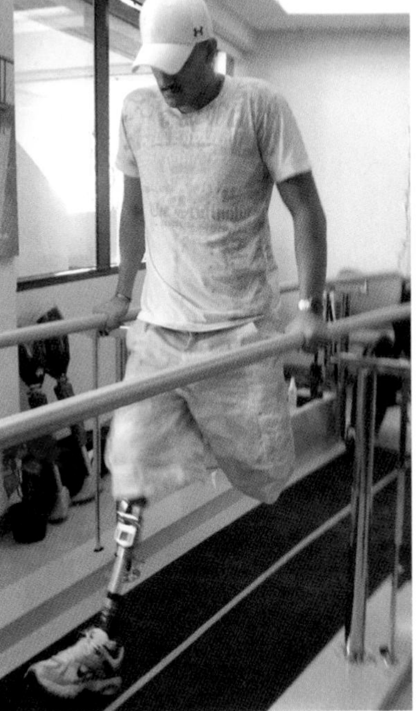

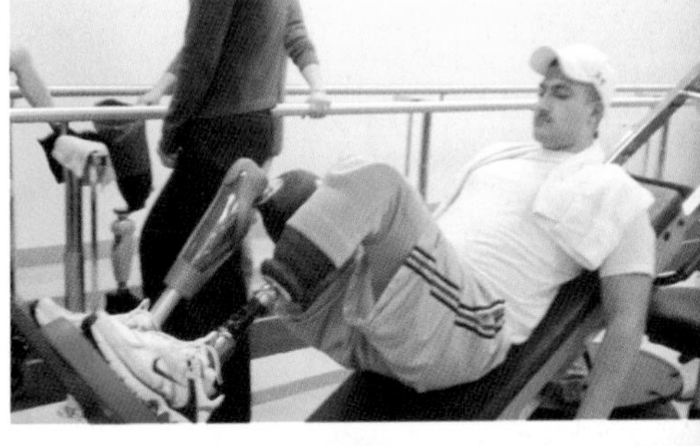

Top left: Two champions, one real, one fictional . . . Gabe and Rocky. Kayla Martinez. *Top center and top right:* Gabe giving his new legs a workout. Kayla Martinez. *Right:* Gabe running on the blades. Kayla Martinez. *Bottom:* Three heroes . . . Trey Humphrey, Gabe Martinez, Carlos Garcia. Lindsey Humphrey

Left: Gabe and Kayla still smiling. *Kayla Martinez. Right:* Gabe (center) at Denver's Rock 'n' Roll Marathon. *Kayla Martinez*

When Gabe and Kayla returned in May for her graduation from college, they stayed until her dad died on May 28, 2011. Thinking about her dad and how he suffered in those final months still brings tears to her eyes.

The couple is moving forward, continuing a journey few have traveled. Their family is growing; Kayla gave birth to Madelynn Grace soon after they moved to Colorado.

Gabe, who picked up sergeant before medically retiring, loves his tattoos, which reflect his optimism and faith. Among them are Philippians 4:13, "I can do all things through Him who gives me strength," and "Tough Times Don't Last But Tough Marines Do."

Though proud of the Purple Heart he received, Gabe calls it "a marksmanship badge for the other side. The Taliban got me." But you won't hear many complaints coming from this warrior, who says with a smile, "Knowing God has given me a second chance leaves little room to complain about anything."

6

NO REGRETS

Jesse and Kelly Cottle

Each bump in the road hurt. Unfortunately, in Afghanistan every road had bumps—lots of them. Considering his medical condition, Staff Sergeant Jesse Cottle, a six-year veteran of the Marine Corps, assumed the pain would be much greater but his body was still somewhat numb from the explosion. Without the help of Navy Corpsman Woody Ender and Gunnery Sergeant Kevin Brown applying tourniquets and stopping the flow of blood, things would have been much different.

Jesse and Kelly coming in from a swim. *Mark Feinauer*

Moments earlier a metal detector cleared the path and two Marines stepped on the same spot where Jesse's foot subsequently landed, detonating a pressure-plate IED, hurling him high into the air. He was a trained EOD technician and knew this was a powerful blast. As he was landing he figured he was missing some body parts; he was hoping for just a foot or maybe a leg below the knee. An accomplished pianist and an extreme-sports enthusiast, panic was not

Top: Navy Hospital Corpsman Woody Ender, Gunnery Sergeant Kevin Brown, Staff Sergeant Jesse Cottle, and Staff Sergeant Patrick Hilty in front of a Russian tank in Afghanistan. *Jesse Cottle. Bottom:* Jesse and the EOD team sheltered by an armored Humvee during a controlled detonation. *Jesse Cottle*

The team in front of their armored vehicle. *Jesse Cottle*

Jesse on guard. *Jesse Cottle*

Waiting for the landlord to return. *Jesse Cottle*

part of his makeup. He let the training take over. Remaining calm, he reached for a tourniquet. Before he could apply it, Woody, Kevin, and Staff Sergeant Patrick Hilty rushed to his aid. It was then he learned it was more than a foot; it was both legs.

As the MRAP raced toward the casualty evacuation point and the waiting Black Hawk medevac helicopter, Jesse experienced a strange peace. He assumed he was going to die. He didn't argue with God or make promises he had no intention of keeping. He did, however, reflect on "regrets." He was twenty-four and a few things came to mind. He regretted he wouldn't get to finish Stephen King's *Dreamcatcher*. He had only about fifty pages to go in the 896-page novel. He could see the book sitting on the wooden bookshelf back at the mud hut compound in Now Zad, where he lived with his EOD teammates. If someone could get him the book and he could live another hour or so he could finish it. But he had a bigger regret. He never met the right girl; the thought of being a husband and father always pleased him. Now it looked like it was never going to happen.

☆ ☆ ☆

After the explosion the doctors at hospitals in Bagram, Landstuhl, Bethesda, and Balboa performed one miracle after another. It went on for months.

The legs were gone but he was alive.

☆ ☆ ☆

Jesse's parents and Kelly Forrester's parents attended the same church in Scottsdale, Arizona. In fact, they were in a Bible study group together. When his parents shared the news about Jesse's injuries, prayers upon prayers were offered and as time progressed the Cottles provided periodic updates on Jesse's condition.

While being treated at Balboa, Jesse spent a weekend with his parents in Phoenix and met the Forresters. They invited Jesse to join them in San Diego in a few weeks to watch their daughter Kelly, who swam at Boise State, compete in an upcoming meet.

Jesse was just up on his new legs. It took the aid of two canes to stabilize the childlike wobble but he made it to the swim meet. He'd never been to one before and wasn't quite sure what to expect. He certainly didn't expect Kelly! She was warming up, racing through the water, when she spotted her parents in the stands. The competition would begin soon but she climbed out of the water to greet her parents and meet Jesse.

Kelly in the lead for Boise State. *Mark Feinauer*

Just engaged. *Bev Forrester*

As she emerged from the water in her one-piece suit, Jesse was captivated. Tall and statuesque, she looked like a model from the latest *Sports Illustrated* swimsuit edition. Only she was the real thing, a record-setting collegiate swimmer. That night he joined the family for dinner and saw her without the goggles and swim cap. It only got better. His reaction: Wow!

Although both were dating others, a friendship began. It evolved into love.

Jesse being congratulated by Brian Meyer and Justin Schmaltstieg after being awarded the Bronze Star with Combat V for valor. Within a year Justin would be dead and Brian grievously wounded. *Mark Feinauer*

For Kelly, it was the man, not the missing legs. The artificial limbs didn't define him. As she explains, "Jesse didn't get to choose whether he wanted to be in this situation, so how could I choose not to be with him because of it? I don't just love Jesse in spite of his injuries, I love him because of them as well. The unique aspects of our relationship are born from the physical limitations Jesse has. It brings a depth to our relationship that wouldn't exist otherwise. There are few better ways to reveal a man's character than to put him in a situation like Jesse's."

Jesse Cottle's bumpy road journey in Afghanistan on July 19, 2009, produced more than he could ever dream. A recipient of a Bronze Star with a Combat V for valor, he no longer has any regrets. He finished the Stephen King novel and he found the right girl!

Kelly Willardson

Jason Hicks

7

SIX-PLUS YEARS

Allan and Carolyn Carpenter

Six years, four months, and three days . . . but who's counting? Carolyn Carpenter was. That's how long her husband, Allan Carpenter, then a Navy lieutenant, was held by the NVA, the North Vietnamese Army.

The "Zoo" was no place for a family outing, nor was the "Hanoi Hilton" a Southeast Asian extended-stay resort. They were, however, two of the places Al Carpenter was imprisoned during his six-plus years in captivity. Isolation, deprivation, and torture were watchwords of the prison system and Al experienced them all.

When her husband was shot down on his 135th combat mission, Carolyn was a young mother of four, the youngest twenty-two months and the oldest seven.

Al and the Carpenter children before his last deployment to Vietnam. *Carolyn Carpenter*

Top: Hundreds of American POWs were held at the Hanoi Hilton. It wasn't a hotel! *National Archives.*
Bottom: U.S. Navy A4E Skyhawks. *U.S. Navy*

On August 21, 1966, Al was on his second deployment to Vietnam when his aircraft was severely damaged by ground fire. With his plane fully engulfed in flames, he was forced to eject a short distance from his ship, the aircraft carrier USS *Franklin D. Roosevelt*. He was plucked from the ocean by a rescue helicopter, returned to the ship, given a shot of whiskey, and told to get some rest. The next morning his was the first aircraft launched. He says, "It's like riding a horse: if you get thrown, you get back on."

A little more than two months later, on November 1, Al was the flight leader for three A4E Skyhawks on an "Iron Hand" photo reconnaissance mission over the ever-dangerous Haiphong Harbor. While attacking a surface-to-air missile site, his plane was hit by antiaircraft fire and he was forced to eject. His wingman confirmed he had been picked up by a North Vietnamese fishing boat.

In Jacksonville, Florida, the carrier's home port, Carolyn received the horrific news that day in a personal visit from the wife of the ship's commanding officer. As gently as possible, Carolyn shared the information with their three older children. Although the families of POWs were asked not to discuss their loved one's POW status, it was impossible to keep the news a secret on a military base. Friends and neighbors rallied, offering support. When their oldest daughter,

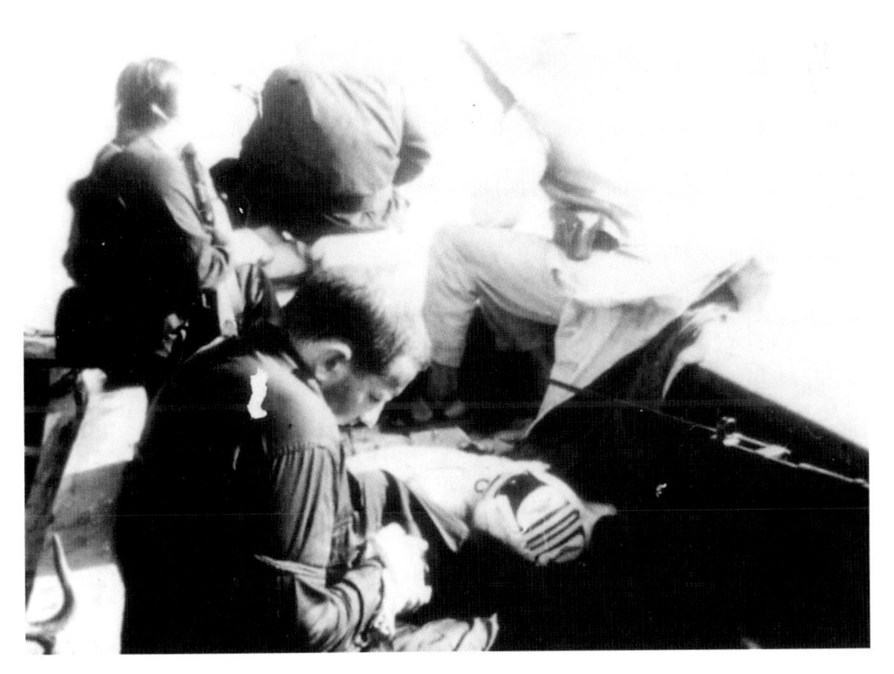

Al Carpenter shortly after his capture by the North Vietnamese. *NVA propaganda photo*

April, returned to school she told her classmates her "dad was in prison" . . . causing some confusion that Carolyn quickly cleared up.

* * *

The next summer, Carolyn and the kids returned to Maine to be closer to both families. There were few secrets in a small town and even though she didn't talk much about Al being a POW, the townspeople knew. She tried to make life as normal as possible but it wasn't easy. Christmas time was always the hardest. Still today a tear comes to her eye as she explains how one year the children remained on the couch, watching her put ornaments on the tree, refusing to participate. "Daddy's not here. We don't want to decorate it."

Communication was almost nonexistent. Her first letter from Al came a year after he was captured and averaged about one a year. Her messages were limited to prepared stationery which when folded made its own envelope. She was limited to just six lines of text. She tried to send "care" packages every other month through the Red Cross. At the time she didn't know it but few ever arrived. One that did continues to bring a smile. She found cans of Cold Duck champagne and included two cans in one of the Red Cross bundles. When it arrived, the prison guard made Al open the package in front of him, as was prison policy. For a reason still unknown to Al, the guard allowed him to empty the contents into his metal cup. Al returned to his cell offering to share the drink but since it was his anniversary his cell mates permitted him to enjoy the full pleasure of the occasion. It may have been the only alcohol consumed by a prisoner at the Hanoi Hilton during the war.

The North Vietnamese defied nearly every international agreement, declaring the men "criminals" rather than prisoners of war, and failed to give an accounting of the men being held. Reports of extensive abuse and torture were classified by the U.S. government. The wives and families had been encouraged to keep a low profile as to the POWs and were assured efforts were being made to seek the prisoners' release. But as years passed with no visible progress, Sybil Stockdale, the wife of James Stockdale, who would later be awarded the Medal of Honor for his heroic efforts as a POW, helped initiate what evolved into the National League of POW/MIA Families. Carolyn participated, along with many other wives and family members, in writing to Congress, newspapers, and various foreign governments seeking humane treatment of those being held. In time treatment improved somewhat as the Nixon administration struggled to gain freedom for those imprisoned.

Through the many years of confinement, hope never diminished. Carolyn knew one day Al would return. That day finally came in 1973. Operation Homecoming saw the return of 591

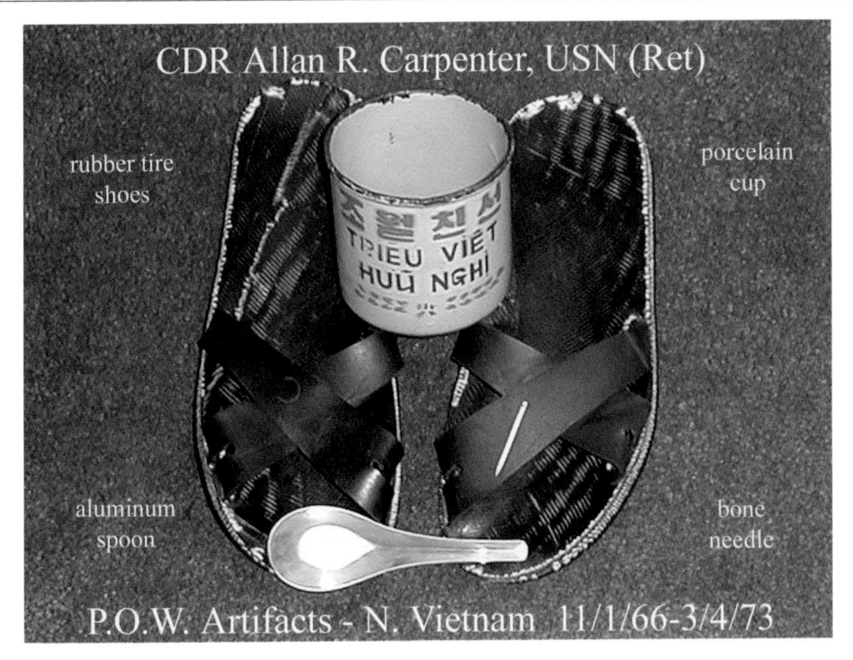

Allan Carpenter

servicemen held in Southeast Asia. They were released in sequence based upon their length of captivity; the first group freed on February 12. Al's release was to come shortly thereafter in the second phase. The anticipation built, as in a matter of days they would be together. Expectations consumed every thought; they yearned to be a family once again. The years of separation were about to be history . . . then negotiations broke down! Questions arose as to if or when Al and the remaining POWs would be released. For Carolyn this was the hardest period of the entire ordeal. Freedom seemed so near but was now elusive.

Finally, on March 4, 1973, the communist government in Hanoi relented and the second group was freed. The family sat around the TV as the networks televised the men exiting the plane in the Philippines. When their son Mark, nine years old, saw his dad walking down the steps he blurted out, "Mom, he looks really young. What happened to you?" It was the next day before Al was able to call, and within days he flew into Boston, where Carolyn waited. After a comprehensive medical examination, he and Carolyn flew to Maine, where the family was reunited. Kelly, who was only twenty-two months old when he was shot down on November 1, 1966, wouldn't leave Al's side, determined to stay close to the daddy she really didn't know.

* * *

Top: POW choir on the way home, 1973. *Allan Carpenter.* *Left:* Al, Carolyn, and the four Carpenter children reunited at last. *Carolyn Carpenter*

Top: With President Richard Nixon at the White House welcome-home on May 24,1973. *Allan Carpenter.*
Bottom: Carolyn and Al Carpenter with Medal of Honor recipient Sammy Davis at the Freedom Alliance Army-Navy weekend, 2012. *Freedom Alliance*

Al wasn't ready to quit even after six years of confinement. He needed to get back to flying . . . to get back on the horse. His heroics before and after being shot down resulted in him being awarded three Silver Stars, the third-highest combat award the Navy offers, and the Legion of Merit. Like most who serve he doesn't view himself as a hero. In fact, he says with a smile, "By some standards, I'm nothing but a 'loser,' having been responsible for the destruction of two of our Navy's expensive war machines, and thereby having made myself unavailable for combat operations for nearly six and a half years!" But he really is a hero.

The family sold the home Carolyn purchased in Maine and moved to Virginia Beach, where Al continued his career, retiring as a commander. Their marriage has lasted as well: more than fifty-six years . . . but who's counting?

☆ ☆ ☆

MICAH AND LUKE'S DAD

With more than a billion users, Facebook, the social networking phenomenon, provides the opportunity to express innermost thoughts to hundreds, even thousands of "friends" you've never met. A recent Pew Research Center study found that 93 percent of all teenagers who use social media have a Facebook account.

Micah Combs is in the majority with her Facebook account but at her high school she is in a very distinct minority. She lives in the Midwest, far from any military base, and her dad is deployed. She may be the only one in her school with a father serving overseas. Two of her Facebook postings speak volumes:

6 months until my birthday
5 months until Christmas
4 months until Thanksgiving
3 months until Halloween

Micah, a champion. *Daniel Combs*

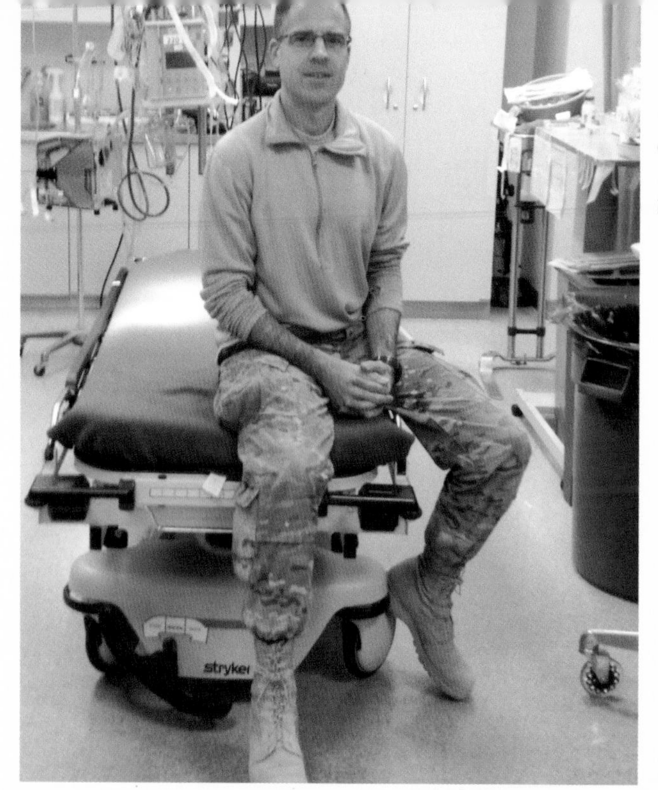

Commander Daniel Combs, Medical Corps U.S. Navy, lifesaver in Afghanistan. *Daniel Combs*

U.S. Navy corpsman treating an Afghan child at a battalion aid station. *USMC Sgt. Jose Soto*

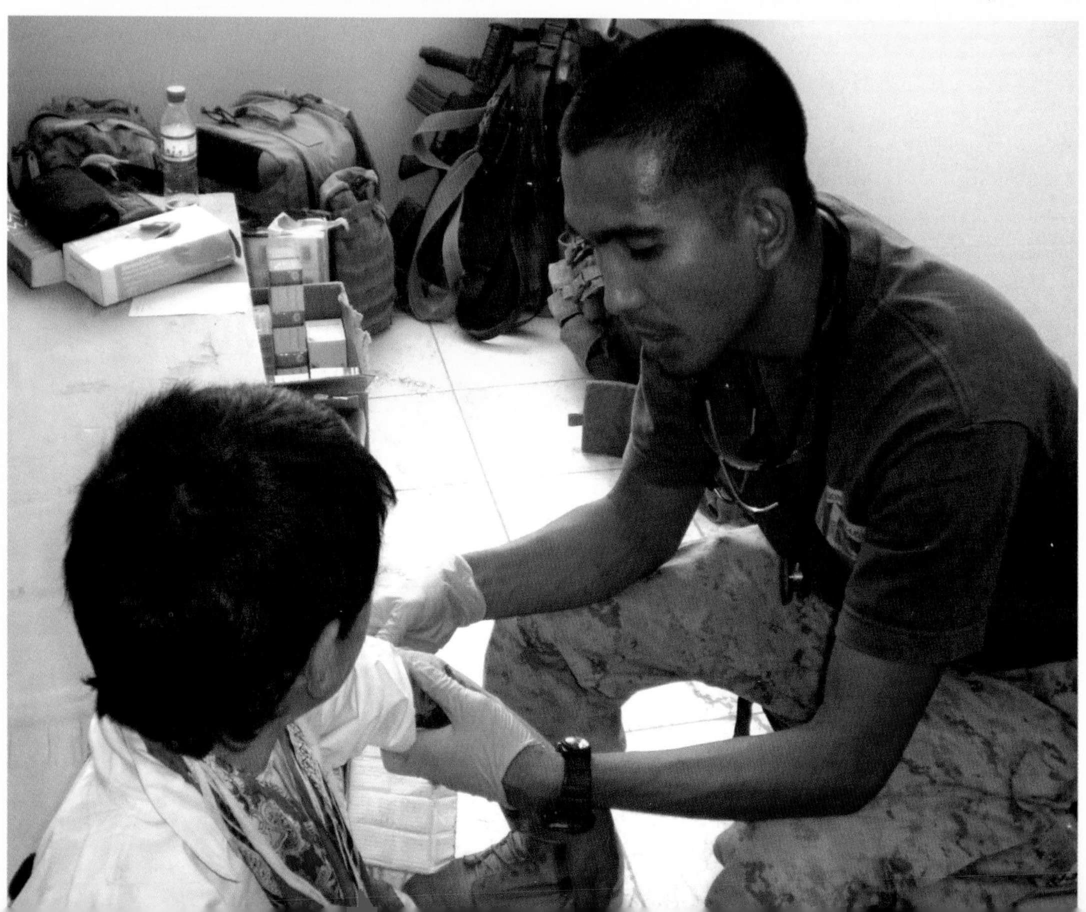

> And less than one month until my daddy leaves for Afghanistan. My daddy won't be here for these events or the next eight months. Please keep him and my family in your prayers. Thanks.

In a later posting she wrote:

> Tomorrow he leaves. I'm gonna miss my daddy. Wish he could stay here with me. I think I am definitely going to be pushed to my limits this year, what with cross-country, starting high school, Dad being gone, and turning fifteen. Dreading the fighting through, but excited to see what God has in store for me at the end.

Navy Commander Daniel Combs's daughter, Micah, is pretty "squared away," as Sailors and Marines like to say. It's hard enough for a teenage girl starting high school to face the challenges everyday life throws at her without the burden of having a father deployed to a combat zone.

But it's also tough on his fifth-grade son, Luke.

The Combs kids. *Daniel Combs*

He misses his dad and a recent letter probably misted an eye or two when Commander Combs opened his mail.

Luke Combs racing for the finish line. *Daniel Combs*

Dear Dad,

How are you doing? I miss you like crazy! Have you saved a lot of people? I bet you are the best doctor there. Basketball is coming very quick. I can't wait till NCAA basketball comes. Maybe the Hoosiers will go and win every single game. I will try to film the NCAA championship when Indiana makes it there. School is also going great. Mrs. Boone is the best teacher in fifth grade. I got straight A's on my report card. It is not the same around here without you! I pray a lot at night because I miss you so much. If you have the time please write back! I miss you like crazy!!!

Love,
Luke

Their dad is a rare breed: a patriot who could have said "enough." As a medical doctor, he left a wife and five children and took a pay cut to serve where few are willing to go. It's been said less than 1 percent of our population has served in the War on Terror, but he did and it could have ended there. He fulfilled his military obligation, which included a combat deployment to Iraq, where he saved lives: American and Iraqi. His youngest son was born ten days before he completed that seven-month deployment. No one would have objected had he simply returned to civilian life. He and his family knew the costs of his service and the potential price of him remaining a reservist.

His own words say it best: "I can hardly explain with words how painful it is to say 'good-bye' to your family for months on end. Young children only know that Daddy isn't there for soccer games, choir performances, bedtime stories, or hugs. But someone has to go. Hopefully someday they will understand why Daddy had to stand that watch and they'll understand that the sacrifice—their sacrifice—was for the greater good."

Our men and women sent in harm's way deserve the best. Micah and Luke's dad is the one you want at that battalion aid station or combat surgical hospital if it's your loved one struggling to survive a terrorist's IED or an insurgent's bullet. Our freedom is the product of sacrifices made by this dad and his family and thousands of others like them who believe in duty, honor, courage, and commitment.

3.5
WOLFPACK
12
22
10
13
23
21
14
11

8

WOLFPACK

It sounds like a grade school riddle . . . what has nine hands, four legs, and dribbles?

Give up? It's the starting lineup of the Wolfpack wheelchair basketball team. Based out of the Naval Medical Center San Diego, the team's roster includes wounded and injured Marines, Soldiers, and Sailors.

Representing a variety of military occupational specialties—infantry, scout-snipers, combat engineers, artillery, and corpsmen—they bring to the basketball court the same drive, dedication, and focus they brought to the battlefield. Theirs is a Cinderella story, one of humble beginnings rising quickly to championship play.

The medical staff at the hospital recognizes the value of recreational activity as it impacts not only the quality of life but also physical and emotional healing. The activities provided range from hunting and fishing to golf, competitive skiing, and hand cycling. With the help of the staff, community volunteers, and nonprofit organizations, service members assigned to the Wounded Warrior Battalion are given unique opportunities to further their rehabilitation and reintegration into the military and civilian world.

When several combat-wounded Marines approached Marla Knox about starting a wheelchair basketball program she knew just where to begin. A certified recreational therapist, she

Facing page: The Wolfpack basketball team. *U.S. Navy*

Brian Meyer pulling in the big one. *Bob Hamer*

had years of experience with wheelchair basketball prior to joining the hospital staff in 2006. She quickly learned the men didn't need much encouragement. The wounded Marines found players whose competitive nature in combat carried over to the court. Although the team was short on experience, in less than a year they were winning nationally recognized tournaments, defeating teams that had been playing together for years.

Jesse Cottle proves you don't need legs to ride a bike. *Kelly Cottle*

Only Marine Sergeant Anthony McDaniel had played basketball beyond high school but his athleticism carried over to the wheelchair game. A triple amputee, he adjusted quickly to grabbing passes with his only hand, doing a slight adjustment of the ball to get a proper grip, then popping three-pointers, all while strapped to a chair.

Neither Sergeant Eric Rodriguez nor Corporal Josue Barron played in high school, unless you count weekend pickup games on the playgrounds of Los Angeles. Each lost a leg in Afghanistan. Josue also lost an eye and Eric has been fighting to salvage the badly wounded remaining leg. Both, however, adjusted well to the chair, demonstrating phenomenal balance and skills, and catching the eye of a college coach who offered them scholarships to play wheelchair basketball at the collegiate level.

But it takes more than three players to make a winning team. Carlos Garcia, Carlos Torres, Marcus Chischilly, Jesse Schag, Jorge Salazar, Ike Blunt, Jhoonar Barrera, Hector Varela, Bill Kiehl, Dan Cashen, and Juan Woidtke provide plenty of strength for their coach, David Rodarte, himself in a chair and a veteran wheelchair basketball player.

The men of Wolfpack represent the finest qualities of our military. The duty, honor, courage, and commitment they demonstrated in service to their country are now on display when they take the court. They could have quit and taken the easy way out, but they triumphed over their individual tragedies and continue to march . . . even though some are without legs.

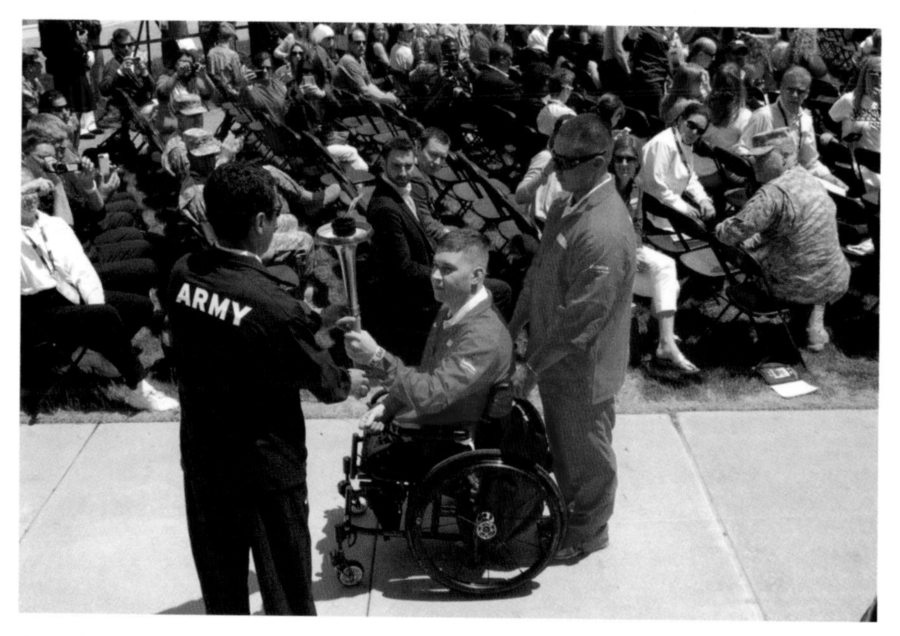

Army Specialist Luis Puertas (ret), USMC Private First Class Artem Lazukin, and USMC Sergeant Eric Rodriguez at the 2013 Warrior Games. *USMC SSgt. Brent Powell*

Left: Eric Rodriguez hitting them long and straight. *U.S. Navy.*
Right: Brian Meyer: Who says you need two legs to snowboard? *U.S. Navy*

Top left: Trey Humphrey on a high-speed downhill. *U.S. Navy. Top right:* Jorge Ortiz keeping warm in a Freedom Alliance ski jacket. *U.S. Navy*

Gabe Martinez: Winter sports are fun when your feet don't get cold. *U.S. Navy*

Below: Jhoonar Barrera. *U.S. Navy Mass Communications Spec Seaman Pyoung K. Yi.*
Right: The bench at a Wolfpack basketball game. *Bob Hamer*

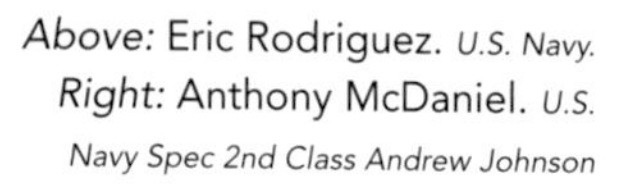
Above: Eric Rodriguez. *U.S. Navy.*
Right: Anthony McDaniel. *U.S. Navy Spec 2nd Class Andrew Johnson*

Josue Barron. *U.S. Navy Mass Communications Spec Seaman Pyoung K. Yi*

Eric Rodriguez. *U.S. Navy*

Marcus Chischilly. *U.S. Navy Mass Communications Spec Seaman Pyoung K. Yi*

9

☆ ☆ ☆

NOT WOUNDED, REDESIGNED

Tim and Connie Lee

Marine Sgt. Tim Lee, American Hero—redesigned—speaking at Liberty University. *Tim Lee*

In 2010, Tim Lee peered out the window of the commercial jetliner and spied the land below. It was dark green and glowing, rich in color, lavish in its definition. His memories of this place were just as colorful but not nearly as pleasant. The war called "Vietnam" began fifty years ago. Few of the Americans who fought there came home to a hero's welcome. There were no ticker-tape

Left: Tim Lee on graduation from Marine Corps ITR (Infantry Training Regiment). *Tim Lee*
Right: Working on a communications building at Hill 327. *Tim Lee*

parades. Family members might say "thank you for your service" but not many others. Many who served came home, took off their uniforms, and tried to forget that period in our history. But Tim Lee couldn't forget. He wanted to remember. The experience shaped his future. He needed to know his fight and the sacrifices he and so many Americans made in Southeast Asia had purpose. He was returning to Vietnam, where catastrophic injuries knocked him down but never knocked him out. He has been fighting the "good fight" ever since.

★ ★ ★

On March 8, 1971, at New York's Madison Square Gardens, Smokin' Joe Frazier and Muhammad Ali, both undefeated heavyweight champions, were only hours from what was billed as boxing's "Battle of the Century." Half a world away in Quang Nam Province, South Vietnam, a real life-and-death struggle was taking place. A nineteen-year-old Marine lay in his own blood and mangled tissue; both legs were gone. Seconds before, he stood six feet tall. Now he would never stand that tall again . . . or would he?

★ ★ ★

The Marines, accompanied by a team of South Korean Marines, were sweeping an abandoned trail, seeking land mines and explosives hidden by the enemy. Bomb craters pitted the landscape as the Marines cautiously proceeded through the knee-high elephant grass. Corporal Tim Lee had the point, several meters ahead of the others. It was a little after 1330 (1:30 in the afternoon in civilian time), when Tim's boot tripped a sixty-pound box mine, a deadly device built to stop tanks and heavy trucks. A 187-pound Marine versus a well-placed box mine is never a fair fight. The bomb won, as a horrendous hell ignited at Tim's feet. Shrapnel seared his body as the earth pitched its unwanted debris toward the skies.

Tim Lee taking a break before heading out on a minesweeping mission. *Tim Lee*

Seconds later, a South Korean Marine stepped on an antipersonnel mine. His foot was gone. A quiet, serene countryside only two klicks from base camp had erupted into chaos. Everything to the front of the squad was a black inferno. Flesh, bone, blood, and shredded bits of uniform were flying in every direction.

Lance Corporal Lee Gore was the first to reach Tim, followed closely by "Doc" and Ray Bertschy, the radio man. Earl Lewis froze in his position, providing security, scanning the horizon for the enemy.

Thinking it was a mortar attack, Ray instinctively grabbed both Tim and the detached boot filled with Tim's lower leg and pulled them into the three-foot crater still smoldering with smoke. Tim's remaining leg, butchered and lifeless, was barely attached to his upper thigh. Everything was showered in blood as the sharp noxious smell of sulfur and charcoal lingered.

Ray got on the radio and called for chopper support. "Knoxville Charlie, Knoxville Charlie, do you read me?"

The other Marines ripped out their personal battle dressings and pressed them against multiple open wounds and what was left of Tim's mauled lower limb. The morphine shot administered by the Navy corpsman did little to ease the pain. "Knoxville Charlie, Knoxville Charlie. JJ, we need two medevacs: one primary and one emergency, over."

In and out of consciousness, Tim could pick up the faint muffled sounds surrounding him and see Lee Gore's black face, wet with tears. Lee, a devout Christian unafraid to demonstrate his faith, prayed aloud, "God, don't let this boy die! Let him live to serve You!"

Tim was on his back passing in and out of darkness as Ray popped yellow smoke marking the LZ (landing zone) for the approaching helicopter. Two Marines, one from the United States and one from South Korea, shared a ride neither had planned on making that day; their immediate destination the USS *Sanctuary* in the Gulf of Tonkin. The roar of the blades, the blast of the radio, and the hot air swirling about the cabin were ghostly sentinels announcing Tim's new normal.

Once aboard the hospital ship, Tim was off-loaded from the helicopter as his detached leg, placed in the chopper by Ray Bertschy, suddenly fell out of the bird onto the flight deck with an ominous *thud.* More thuds would be heard on his journey to live.

The young Marine was rushed into surgery for one of thirteen major surgical procedures that would highlight his medical history. The first doctor to examine him was Dr. Robert Bailey, a skilled Navy surgeon who would become a good friend. He was a miracle man who saved lives. On that day it was Tim's.

* * *

For Tim, the USS *Sanctuary* was a blur of fast-forward memories; the greatest and most severe was pain. He described it as "a raging fire in what little remained of my legs." He recalled the bright lights, whiffs of medicinal alcohol, the excruciating agony of applying multiple compressive bandages, dangling IVs, and the unforgettable arrival of phantom limb pain. And there were the countless nurses, attendants, and corpsmen giving him multiple injections as pain and infection surged throughout his body.

From the ship he was flown to the island of Guam in the South Pacific, where death knocked again as his temperature spiked at 107 degrees. The treatment, alternating between being submerged in ice and wrapped in heated blankets, worked, and within two weeks he was just well enough to be rolled aboard a USAF aero-medical flight and flown to the Philadelphia Naval Hospital for more cutting.

Here he was passed into the care of two young Navy surgeons. Their surgical philosophy, "cut and remove," differed dramatically from Dr. Bailey's. Maybe prizing their new "subject" as a test case, they removed a dramatic amount of flesh and bone. As the infections persisted, the doctors continued to whittle away at the nubs of this former record-setting high school athlete. The box mine had traumatically amputated Tim's right leg below the knee, his left leg just above

(WASHINGTON DC.

DOMESTIC SERVICE		WESTERN UNION TELEGRAM	INTERNATIONAL SERVICE	
Check the class of service desired; otherwise this message will be sent as a fast telegram		W. P. MARSHALL, CHAIRMAN OF THE BOARD — R. W. McFALL, PRESIDENT	Check the class of service desired; otherwise the message will be sent at the full rate	
TELEGRAM			FULL RATE	
DAY LETTER			LETTER TELEGRAM	
NIGHT LETTER			SHORE-SHIP	

NO. WDS.-CL. OF SVC.	PD. OR COLL.	CASH NO.	CHARGE TO THE ACCOUNT OF	TIME FILED
			WASHINGTON D.C.	3/10/71 11:51 E.S.T.

Send the following message, subject to the terms on back hereof, which are hereby agreed to

To MR + MRS. John R. LEE Jr. 1971

Street and No. 200 South Silas Ave.

Care of or Apt. No. — Destination McLEANSBORO, Illinos

A report received this Headquarters reveals that your son Cpl. Timothy E. Lee, U.S.M.C. sustained his injuries on 8th March 1971, in Quang Nam province Republic of Viet Nam when he accidently detonated a hostile explosive device. Your son continues to recieve treatment, aboard the U.S. Naval Hospital ship, U.S.S. Sanctuary, he remains on the very seriously ill list with his prognosis fair. Your anxiety is realized and you are assured that he continues to recieve the best of medical care. You will be kept informed of all significant changes in his condition. His mailing address remains the same.

(Signed) Leonard F. Chapman Jr. Gen. U.S.M.C. Commandant of the Marine Corps.

The telegram Tim Lee's parents received notifying them he was wounded in action.

the knee. After multiple surgeries only three inches remained on his right and eleven inches on his left.

The prospect of walking again was erased. Despair overtook him. It was as if he was on an elevator going down past the realm of hope; down past any kind of a credible future, to an unmarked damp subterranean floor of no return. The unwarranted surgeries left him a permanent tenant for the cold steel of a wheelchair.

For the first couple of months in Philadelphia he was extremely weak. The simplest tasks—rolling over, sitting up, or reaching for a food tray—seemed impossible. The first time he attempted to use the commode was horrifying. Fear gripped him even in the most ordinary functions of life. Transitioning from leading a squad of Marines on a deadly mine sweep to being totally dependent upon a female nurse to put a straw in his mouth was humiliating.

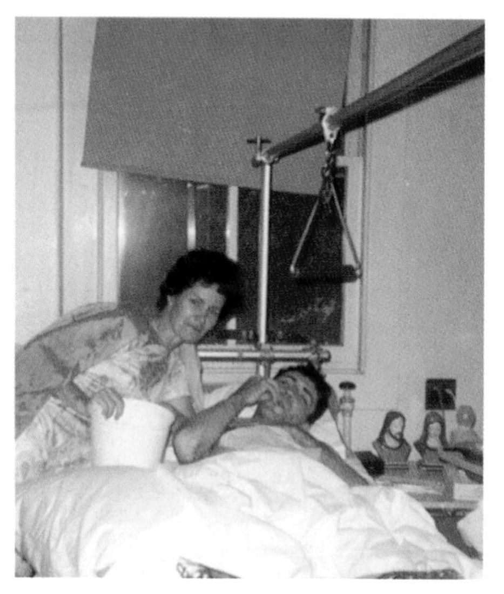

With his mom, Wanda Lee, at the Philadelphia Naval Hospital.

Unlike the military hospitals of today, where the wounded have private rooms, Philadelphia Naval had open wards with dozens of beds lining each wall. All that was separating Tim from everyone else on the floor was a thin cotton curtain. Watching men who were writhing in pain after coming back from horrible surgeries was a daily numbing experience. He could hear every sound, every conversation coming from the beds around him. "I'm sorry to inform you . . ." was a common communication. "No, you won't be able to do that again, Sergeant." Everything was negative, as the hopes of so many physically damaged men were dashed by those who had to tell them the truth.

Severe depression engulfed him. It threatened to kill his spirit as it invaded the recesses of his mind and emotions. It blocked his ability to reason and to believe in the future, jettisoning dreams and purpose. As Tim explained it, "Call it depression, despondency, pity, fear, anger, frustration, whatever you want to call it. This evil pirate was attempting to assassinate the virtues of faith, trust, belief, dignity, and the realm of possibility. For a fleeting moment I forgot the words of scripture *'I can do ALL THINGS through Christ which strengthen me'* (Philippians 4.13) and what Jesus said, *'All things are possible to him that BELIEVETH'* (Mark 9.23). I was raised to believe there was a divine purpose for all of us! That nothing happens by fate or luck of the draw. We're not abandoned to mere blind circumstance."

Through his faith he found hope. He came to believe life's story was written with hardship, with trial and reality, with pain, and with catastrophic detours. It was not just about the Marines, or war, or the terrifying traumas that can befall a serviceman. It was about a far greater reality and destiny. He was not expendable collateral damage, a lump of useless flesh. He was an emerging champion: a winner, a fighter, a special agent in the hand of God for an amazing new purpose. He would still be at war, but his theater of operations had changed dramatically. He came to realize he hadn't been wounded; he had been re-created . . . *redesigned.*

Tim believed there was a prevailing power that overruled what men, doctors, or naysayers said or thought. The X-ray didn't tell the whole story. No matter what the briefing said, no matter what was written on the chart—there was a higher authority! He observed the other amputees, some of them in far worse shape and some not as bad. Many of them got their wedding rings back from their wives. He watched these heroes weep uncontrollably. He heard them scream in the night after another surgery. He saw them convulse through horrifying nightmares. Men died in their racks because they quit; they gave up . . . they surrendered to defeat or fear; they succumbed and they departed this world. They were amazing Marines, many of whom could have lived and loved and hoped and pressed on. But the courage and commitment they showed on the battlefield were left on that same battlefield, felled by devastating injuries.

There was a single moment in the Philadelphia Naval Hospital when Tim Lee made a decision: "Defeat will not be my story! I will be the best person I can be, I will *not* die here, physically or emotionally. I will survive; I will go on; I will live life to the fullest. Pity will not be a word in my dictionary, nor will I allow others to feel pity for me. There is something for me to do. It isn't finished!"

Through all of this there was slow improvement. He began to gain strength. His body began to rebuild itself. He had to learn all over again how to move and maneuver; this time without legs. The constant burn of pain was the greatest nemesis; it was wrenching, unbearable pain that wouldn't go away without a strong injection of medication. Changing the dressings on his wounds was excruciating, with no words adequately defining that horrible process.

His postwar battlefield became the hospital. Once again it was life or death as he drew a line in the sand. He chose life. Few believed he would survive as the medical odds were against him.

In July, the doctors began talking about a major surgical procedure Tim would need in the near future but they agreed Tim could go home for two weeks to McLeansboro, Illinois, where his father pastored a church of about two hundred. When his parents visited him for his birthday earlier in the month they said a new family began attending the church. Tim's mom smiled when she mentioned they had a daughter, Connie, Tim's age.

Back home with Dad and Mom, John and Wanda Lee. *Tim Lee*

Tim flew home, arriving on Saturday. He knew he would be loved and accepted by his family but was concerned about the reception he would receive in public. Vietnam was a sensitive political issue and veterans, even combat-wounded veterans, weren't always perceived as heroes. On Sunday morning he attended church with his family. As he wheeled into the Sunday school classroom, he spied a beautiful young lady sitting by herself. Her shoulder-length brown hair accented a smile that captured his heart. For Tim, it really was love at first sight as he rolled toward Connie and introduced himself. Much of his remaining time at home on leave was spent with her.

McLeansboro was a small town and though Connie didn't know Tim, she knew of him. She and her family started attending the church after Tim left for the Marine Corps but she was aware of his injuries from others in the congregation. The entire church had been praying for Tim even before they heard the news of his crippling wounds. Connie knew and respected the family, so when she saw him that Sunday, it was as if they had already met. She knew immediately the injuries he suffered in Vietnam didn't define him; his faith did.

She had been dating someone else, but when Tim asked her out while he was home on leave, she agreed with little hesitation. When asked what attracted her to him, she said, "He was fun to be with and treated me like a lady. Besides, he was a Christian and looked great in a uniform." The power of a man in uniform!

When Tim returned to Philadelphia Naval for continued medical treatment, he and Connie exchanged letters and the occasional phone call. Even more than forty years later he still has every letter she sent him. Each letter, even if only a couple of paragraphs, conveyed hope.

But soon after arriving at the hospital he received devastating news; the worst news of the entire ordeal. The doctors had been unable to stem the bone infection in what remained of his right leg. While sedated and lying in his bed, he received a visit from the young doctors, the "cutters," as he called them. They explained they were going to do another procedure on Monday. Tim wasn't quite awake and nodded, not understanding the full impact of the conversation. A short time later, his favorite nurse walked in. With uncharacteristic tears streaming down her cheeks, she explained the surgeons planned to remove his right hip; a procedure known as hip disarticulation. At that time with limited medical options, it meant he would never "sit" in the upright position again. He would spend the rest of his natural life on his back or his stomach. After receiving the news, he immediately wheeled down to the end of the ward and used the pay phone to call his dad. He could barely speak as both he and his dad wept at the shocking pronouncement. His father tried to provide comfort and reassurance, telling Tim he would do what he could. Tim placed his faith in God, but this news rocked him to the core. He would rather die than spend his life prone in bed. His father immediately called the hospital, and because of his insistence the operation, a hip disarticulation scheduled for the next Monday, was canceled.

Each Monday the men on the ward, all amputees, attended what they called "stump rounds," a process where the patients went before the doctors and had their treatment and prognosis discussed. On the Monday of the canceled surgery, Dr. Robert Bailey, who had just been transferred to the hospital, was present for stump rounds. When Tim's case was presented, Dr. Bailey introduced himself as the first doctor who treated him on the hospital ship. After reviewing the file, Dr. Bailey was incensed at the treatment Tim had received. Throwing the clipboard, Dr. Bailey announced he would take over Tim's care.

There was another operation, but rather than removing the hip, Dr. Bailey cleaned up the wound and put the young Marine on a new antibiotic, never removing any more of the limb. Tim's response to the treatment was positive and within two weeks he was preparing to go home . . . another miracle.

On November 12, 1971, Tim left the Philadelphia Naval Hospital—*fully alive.* His problems weren't over. There were many, many unknowns, but he had hope. Now at 110 pounds, up from the eighty he weighed at his lowest point, he was able to move himself in the wheelchair, feed himself, take care of his personal needs, and within a matter of weeks he would be driving his own vehicle and living life again.

As the commercial jet roared from the tarmac, Philadelphia was suddenly below and then behind him. Not everything had gone his way. But in his mind he was leaving the past below. This was the beginning of a new life. On the flight home he thought about how he would greet people; he pondered how he would respond to their welcomes, their comments, their stares. It would not be easy; there would be many adjustments, many surprises, many learning experiences to come.

He returned to southern Illinois and the welcoming arms of his family *and* Connie, who accompanied Tim's parents to the airport. Their relationship grew. Connie admits some of her friends questioned why she would date a double amputee, but once they met Tim, their opinions changed. Once they saw beyond the wheelchair, they found the man she found, a man of character and conviction.

On April 28, 1972, they were married and prepared for a new journey and all that God had in store for them. Like many newlyweds they had little in terms of material possessions. Connie was still in school working toward her degree and Tim was collecting a small disability check. He recalled one day he headed out of town to a strawberry farm. Plopping down in the fields and maneuvering with only his arms hopping from row to row on his fists, he picked forty quarts of strawberries. A surprised Connie returned home from school that evening, and love prevailed as she postponed studying for a test to clean and prepare forty quarts of strawberries before they spoiled.

It was soon thereafter he found a job at Western Union but God was nudging him to do more with his gifts and talents. Tim was called to full-time ministry in January 1973. He and

Tim wanted to be standing when he and Connie married. The prosthetics were painful and proved impractical. The prosthetics didn't last . . . the marriage did.

Connie pastored a church for five years before more nudging from God . . . ministry as a full-time evangelist. With three children, the family toured the country in a recreational vehicle for four years before settling in Garland, Texas, where Tim Lee Ministries is headquartered. Married more than forty years, he and Connie continue to provide hope and inspiration to those they touch.

Tim's faith provided the strength for his recovery. He believes there is a purpose for each of us, a reason why we're on this planet. For Tim, Vietnam didn't interrupt that purpose, it defined his mission. From the first day he returned home to Illinois his mind became totally focused on what God's purpose was for him. From that moment on he has never looked back. He and Connie have traveled more than six million miles: over the road and in the air, visiting churches, youth camps, patriotic rallies, and hospitals. Tim has talked of hope in convention centers, arenas, town halls, public parks, and on university campuses. He has spoken face-to-face with hundreds of thousands of people and challenged a generation to overcome any obstacle, any challenge set before them. Even without legs he stands tall!

Left: A surprise reunion with Lee Gore in 1984. When Tim was wounded twelve years earlier, Gore was the Marine who prayed, "God, don't let this boy die! Let him live to serve You." *Tim Lee. Right:* On a fishing trip in Alaska. *Tim Lee*

Tim Lee's observations about his return to Vietnam in 2010 parallel my own in 1993 and 2006. We both had the opportunity to meet former allies and enemies on the battlefields where we were wounded. We went to places where we had lost friends and experienced the horrors of war. And the Vietnamese we encountered on return, whether in the north where we bombed them or in the south where we abandoned them, were uniformly glad to see us—once they figured out we were Americans and not Russians.

Tim and I both served in I Corps—the northernmost provinces of the Republic of Vietnam—a country that no longer exists. In April 1975, after U.S. troops pulled out, the nation we fought to defend was invaded, conquered, and subjugated by Ho Chi-Minh's North Vietnamese Army. The aftermath was an unmitigated catastrophe for the people of the south. Millions of them died or fled. The term "boat people" was created to describe the refugees. Tens of thousands of those who stayed spent years in "reeducation camps."

Decades after this disaster, when Tim and I prepared to return, some said to us: "Why would you want to go there? It was so long ago and such a waste." In the 1960s and 1970s when we were in Vietnam, our Marines often described someone who was killed—friendly or enemy—as "wasted."

Few of those asking "Why go there?" had been to Vietnam. They did not lose someone in "The War"—did not have to wait patiently while someone they loved was there. Nor had they left something of themselves in that faraway place so very long ago. Those who had done these things did not ask, "Why go back?" They understood.

* * *

Tim and I learned there is something therapeutic about "going back." Years before, we both lost friends, comrades, and something of ourselves in Vietnam. It was there, in the midst of war, we put aside forever any illusions of youthful innocence. Returning to Vietnam was a catalyst for chasing out the last of those demons. Anyone who doesn't believe in demons has never really been to war.

For Tim, what began when he was grievously wounded on March 8, 1971, was completed in 2010 during the encounters he had with the children of those we fought to defend. He found no bitterness in the Vietnamese people he met. Though few of them were even born at the time, they knew why Marine Sergeant Tim Lee had come so many years ago—to offer them the hope of Liberty. They saw, understood, and appreciated the sacrifice he made on their behalf—even if some of our own countrymen could not.

Oliver North and legendary Marine John Ripley, Navy Cross recipient, in Dong Ha, Vietnam, 2006. He understood. *Gregory Johnson, FOX News*

With the one-legged NVA veteran to whom I gave my glasses in 2006. *Gregory Johnson, FOX News*

For me, that moment came in 2006 with our FOX News *War Stories* team while poring over a map with a one-legged North Vietnamese Army veteran. In 1969 we were young officers and enemies during a battle in which both of us were wounded—he far worse than I. In 2006, as I plotted "friendly" and "enemy" dispositions on my fading laminated map, he confessed through our interpreter, "I am sorry sir, but my eyes are poor. I cannot see the terrain features."

Without thinking I handed him my inexpensive reading glasses—the kind we can buy for a few dollars in any American pharmacy. The effect was immediate. He suddenly exclaimed, "I can see!" and grabbed my map and grease pencil, making notations about how the gunfight looked from his side of the bloody engagement.

* * *

In 1969 we tried to kill each other. We both lost comrades we revered and we left the battlefield wounded. But this time when we parted, he took with him every pair of reading glasses my producers and I could find in my field kit. I, after all, had three sets of prescription lenses.

The long-retired North Vietnamese officer had lost his leg serving in his army. He had a single crutch, but no prosthetic limb. Age and privation made him nearly blind, but he had no glasses to help him see. Six years after he was disabled, his nation's army vanquished the nation we went to defend. Yet this former enemy soldier bore no animus or arrogance. As we parted he said, "I am now a Christian. Thank you."

Was it worth it to have gone to Vietnam the first time? Yes. Was it worth going back? Absolutely.

Tim Lee is not alone in believing it is possible to be "redesigned" by battle—and reconciliation.

☆ ☆ ☆

EPILOGUE

Tomorrow

This book is about celebration, not devastation. It's about men and women and even children who triumphed over their individual tragedies. Not one is asking for your pity, nor should any be given, but I hope after reading their stories you are inspired by the warrior spirit alive in the men and women and their families who have served and continue to serve this great nation. Any old mariner will tell you, "No good sailor is made on calm seas." Our greatest strengths come as we persevere through our most difficult battles. Those featured in this book have faced tragedy, known struggle, and yet have persevered. They are stronger because of the battle.

I've seen death, destruction, and dismemberment in the jungles of Vietnam, where I served nearly fifty years ago, and on today's battlefields embedded with our servicemen and -women. I consider myself a tough guy, yet one of the hardest things I do is walk into the hospital room of the recently wounded, of someone I saw "whole" a few weeks ago, and now view the devastating injuries recently suffered. I have met men and women, some still teenagers, who will be scarred for life, yet I am emboldened by their courage. I admit to sometimes choking back tears.

It's tough not to "get emotional" when a young boy, only three or four, the son of a decorated Marine killed in combat before the child was born, approaches and asks, "Are you my daddy?" Even for a hardened warrior, that's a difficult moment. For me, it brings to the forefront the sacrifices a few have made for many.

I've been truly blessed to spend most of my life in the company of heroes, many suffering from devastating and life-altering combat wounds. Through the efforts of Freedom Alliance, I've spent time hunting and fishing with these heroes. I've shared dinner and drinks with them, sometimes in fancy restaurants, more often over campfires. Despite their setbacks, I've listened as they've laughed—yes, laughed—retelling tales of their injuries in a way only a combat veteran can tell, with self-deprecating heroism. They've joked about their latest prosthetics and challenged each other to feats of handicap strengths. These heroes ask for nothing, not even recognition, certainly not sympathy. They are anonymous warriors who swore before God to protect this nation against all enemies, foreign and domestic. They answered the call after 9/11with more than a bumper sticker; they answered offering up their lives. They didn't worry about pension plans or entitlements. They understood then as they understand now, our nation is at war with a foe who will never be satisfied until we surrender or die.

Most of the men and women we've featured in this book are amputees, but it wasn't what each lost that captured our attention. It was the optimism and graciousness Bob Hamer and I found in each one we met. Their lives have been changed forever. Their scars may never disappear but these heroes, who are owed so much by this nation, expressed gratitude to us for telling their story. They weren't seeking to place their lives on a pedestal, but to share their message of hope. In fact, few believe themselves to be a hero and would have preferred anonymity, but there was no real and honest way to tell these stories without identifying them.

I question whether we as a nation have become numb to the War on Terror, a war that has been buried on the back pages of almost every newspaper, behind the latest Hollywood scandal, economic news, or political infighting. For many, the war is an afterthought. It no longer fits neatly into a comfortable personal agenda. Too few are touched by this war, with only a small percentage knowing anyone serving. Many Americans prefer to just move on, retreat before the problem is resolved, and blindly hope somehow the jihadists bent on destroying this nation will focus their efforts elsewhere. But for those featured in this book the war is all too real.

They have been in the arena, not up in the stands criticizing the players on the field. They will live with the scars of this battle forever, as will their families. Yet not once in my time with these warriors have I heard even a whimper, never a "woe is me." Even those who will never walk again yearn for the chance to get back to the fight. They knew when they took the oath of enlistment there was no expiration date.

In the words of Heracleitus, the ancient Greek philosopher-soldier:

EPILOGUE

For every one hundred men in battle;
Eighty should never be there;
Ten are nothing more than targets;
Nine are good soldiers;
Ah but the one;
One is a Warrior and he will lead the others home.

* * *

I've often asked myself, What makes a warrior? Why do some men run to the sound of gunfire and others retreat? In a fight-or-flight situation, why will some stand their ground, but others flee? Is there a warrior gene?

It is more than mere indoctrination or training, because in the heat of battle trained men have fled. It is more than peer pressure, because men standing alone have faced great odds and never flinched. There is a warrior ethos that can be taught but in some it seems to be part of their very fabric. We find it in our military and first-responders.

Each of these heroes is a volunteer who knew the risk when taking the oath yet chose to serve when the nation asked, just as those in previous generations answered the call. These men and women have willingly put their lives on the line without hesitation.

I've learned in combat, as I've learned in life, bad things happen in bad places, yet the men and women we've featured in this book didn't get to pick the evil that attacked them and their families. They did, however, choose how they would respond to death, dismemberment, and disability. Rather than flee, they chose to fight. And fight they did, overcoming great odds. They are America's warriors.

We sleep under the blanket of freedom because members of this generation have decided this nation and our way of life are worth preserving. Remember them today, but even more importantly, remember them tomorrow; remember that small percentage, who have chosen to defend us, who have taken the oath, who continue to serve in places we can't pronounce or find on a map. May we never forget the sacrifices represented in these stories of AMERICAN HEROES.

These heroes forfeited the comforts of home, the affection of loved ones and went into harm's way for endless months in some of the most difficult and dangerous places on Earth.

—OLIVER NORTH

GLOSSARY

ALP Afghan Local Police
ANP Afghan National Police
COC Combat Operations Center
Eagle, Globe, and Anchor insignia of the U.S. Marine Corps
EOD Explosive Ordnance Disposal
ETT Embedded Training Team
FOB Forward Operating Base
Gunny nickname for Marine gunnery sergeant
Humvee High Mobility Multipurpose Wheeled Vehicle
IED Improvised Explosive Device
LZ Landing Zone
MARSOC Marine Corps Forces Special Operations Command
Medevac Medical Evacuation
MIA Missing in Action
MOS Military Occupational Specialty
MRAP Mine Resistant Ambush Protected armored fighting vehicle
MRE Meal, Ready-to-Eat
NATO North Atlantic Treaty Organization
NCO Non-Commissioned Officer in the military service
PAO Public Affairs Officer
PB Patrol Base
POW Prisoner of War
RCT Regimental Combat Team
ROTC Reserve Officer Training Corps
RPG Rocket-Propelled Grenade
SAPI Small Arms Protective Insert
UAV Unmanned Aerial Vehicle; reconnaissance aircraft operated by remote control
UGR Unitized Group Rations
USO United Service Organizations

These American heroes are all volunteers—part of the brightest, best-educated, best-trained, and most combat-experienced military force the world has ever known.

—OLIVER NORTH

Index

MILITARY DESIGNATIONS

Italicized numbers indicate pages with illustrations

Greater love hath no man than this, that a man lay down his life for his friends (John 15:13 KJV). These heroes gave their limbs and lives to offer strangers the hope of freedom.

—OLIVER NORTH

NAMES

Italicized numbers indicate pages with illustrations

PLACES

Italicized numbers indicate pages with illustrations

GENERAL

Italicized numbers indicate pages with illustrations

Freedom Alliance

HEROES SCHOLARSHIPS

For the Children of America's Fallen Heroes

The Freedom Alliance Scholarship Fund honors American military personnel who have been killed or permanently disabled in service to our nation by providing educational scholarships for their dependent children.

Since 1990, Freedom Alliance has awarded millions of dollars in college scholarships to the sons and daughters of fallen U.S. Soldiers, Sailors, Airmen, Guardsmen, and Marines. These grants further education and remind all that their parents' sacrifice will never be forgotten by a grateful nation.

SUPPORT OUR TROOPS

Serving Those Who Serve in America's Armed Forces

The Freedom Alliance Support Our Troops program provides direct financial and other assistance to active-duty military personnel and their families. First priority is given to those recuperating from wounds and injuries, and to their dependents.

Through relationships with military and veterans' hospitals and rehabilitation facilities, Freedom Alliance provides emergency grants to families enduring financial hardship while a member of our Armed Forces recovers from wounds, injuries, or sickness suffered in the line of duty.

The Freedom Alliance "Gifts from Home" project ships thousands of care packages to service members deployed overseas throughout the year. Here on the homefront, we provide gifts and sponsor activities for the spouses and children of deployed personnel.

Our Healing Heroes program offers "Hero Holiday" vacations for injured military members and their families and "Hero Hunts," fishing retreats and outdoor activities to aid in rehabilitation.

Freedom Alliance, founded in 1990 by Lieutenant Colonel Oliver North, USMC (Ret.), and Lieutenant General Edward Bronars, USMC (Ret.), is a nonprofit 501(c)(3) charitable and educational organization dedicated to advancing America's heritage of freedom by honoring and encouraging military service, defending the sovereignty of the United States, and promoting a strong national defense.

For more information or to donate, contact:

FREEDOM ALLIANCE

22570 Markey Court, Suite 240

Dulles, VA 20166-6919

Phone: 800-475-6620

www.freedomalliance.org

www.facebook.com/FreedomAlliance

★ **"LEST WE FORGET"** ★